Build CONFIDENCE
and SELF-ACCEPTANCE

UNDERSTANDING
SELF
WORTH

KAREN C. EDDINGTON

D1295177

Dedication

To: My Kids
No matter if you are in my home
or in my heart

Centered Publishing
An extension of Inspire Zeal
Centered, Inc

ISBN 13: 978-0-9816162-4-7
ISBN 10: 0-9816162-4-0

Printed in the United States of America
For more information on this work visit
www.kareneddington.com

Contents

My name is Anecia. I have red hair and blue eyes. I stand four feet ten and a half inches tall. Don't forget the half. I come from a family of six. I am the oldest of four girls. My sisters are my best friends. I never laugh harder than when I am with them. I love country music. I am a sucker for Snickers and snicker doodles. I believe in treating others the way you want to be treated. I believe in always being honest. I want to fix up an old house with a wraparound porch. I want to live happily ever after. I want to make a difference.

As a young girl I would watch my friends highlight and change their hair color. I was never allowed. I was told my natural color is beautiful and rare. One you cannot get from a bottle.

When I was a sophomore in high school I made the cheerleading squad. Having somebody do my hair and makeup on team picture day made me feel like a celebrity. All of the girls had bouncy curls and dark smoky eye makeup. I wanted to look like that too. Unfortunately, my fine red hair and fair skin was no match. My hair laid flat. My makeup looked like a child who had gotten into their mom's makeup and used way too much of all the wrong colors. When I looked in the mirror I didn't look like a celebrity at all. In that moment I felt out of place, like I wasn't really part of the team. I looked around at these confident, beautiful young women, then I looked at myself.

Struggles go beyond high school. As a new mom, I am constantly comparing my parenting to other women with babies the same age as mine. I am always considering what I might be doing wrong. The moment I found out I was having a baby girl my thoughts were, "How am I going to teach her to be a strong, independent, confident woman? How am I going to teach her about self-worth?" It's never going to be easy. She will face many challenges, as I did and still do. Everybody parents differently and I realize what works for others may not work for me.

I realize now that I am unique. My red hair and fair skin set me apart from others.

Karen Eddington was my high school cheerleading coach and after graduation I spent time working with her at her outreach center. Learning about self-worth is important because it is a constant battle. At any age, we are struggling with comparisons and self-doubt. There is always something to learn. Karen has taught me so much about what self-worth means. I have learned the meaning of unique and how it's ok to be different and to stand out from a crowd. You can learn that and much more from Karen.

-Anecia Jensen

I'm hard on myself.
I'm not happy when
I look in the mirror.
I will never be good enough.
People are judging me.
I'm not at peace.
I don't feel good about myself.

I wish I knew how to change it.

Chapter 1

You Matter

Picture yourself surrounded by five thousand people. Look around. What do you see? What do you feel?

I wish you could have experienced the roar of the crowd in the arena. Every seat in the dome stadium was filled. Over five thousand spectators, competitors, and industry professionals were attending the national high school cheerleading competition in Florida.

When you are surrounded by this many people, do you ever feel insignificant, like you don't really matter? Is it easy for you to feel lost? It was a competition, there were cheerleaders, there were judges, and based on the stereotypes the environment has enough factors to make even a zit-free-prom-queen-swimsuit-model question herself.

Among the thousands of people you could see teams in warm-ups grouped together in the stands. There were families who traveled from cities across the country waiting in anticipation for awards. There were people holding cameras, people talking, people eating nachos, staff members managing the event, and even the bored child playing with the bleacher seat. It smelled like hair spray and concession stand popcorn.

If you were to look side to side, you would see well-dressed mothers, professional coaches, sporty cheerleaders carrying uniform bags, strong yell leaders, and beautiful teens representing cities from across the United States. At the back of the room there was a judges' platform with black curtains, where a group of professional-looking people were busy calculating final scores. Five thousand, that's a lot of people in one place.

At the front of the room was a stage consisting of blue foam mats. Standing to the side of the spotlight, feeling the heat of the lights, were seventeen students, lined together. Zoom in. See them wait in the purple and black uniforms, with smiles, to hear their name called.

These seventeen students are my kids. I was their cheerleading coach. This is my most vivid memory of being surrounded by five thousand people.

Backtrack to the 2005 spring cheerleading tryouts at Box Elder High School. The gym is filled with over forty hopeful students, waiting for an opportunity to be a part of the team. Amid all the people, one girl, a courageous blonde soccer player steps forward. She turns in her tryout packet and nervously smiles. She was leaving her comfort zone at the onset of her senior year to try something new. She along with fifteen girls and one boy made the team.

As soon as tryouts are over, the team of seventeen students begins practicing. Summer camp, parades, homecoming, and games become part of their life. There are significant moments like delivering Popsicles to rival fans sitting in the sun, singing on the bus, surviving cold football games, and redoing an entire routine because of an outbreak of the flu. There are memories of hard work, sincere belly laughter, and even inside jokes about sweat. Have you ever heard of "swack"? It's the code word for sweat that drips down your back.

Right from tryouts I noticed something different about this group of students. They invited rivals, people who they should be gossiping about, to be friends with them. They were kind. They supported people at school and in the community. They let go of the cheerleader stereotype. Without the team knowing about it, I put together an entry for the American School Spirit Awards.

In December, while sitting in the gym for early morning practice the team learns they have been named the 2005 American School Spirit Award winners. A major cheerleading association had selected these seventeen students to travel to Florida. While standing on the blue competition mats in the heat of the lights they received a standing ovation in front of five thousand people for their leadership and ability to break stereotypes.

Zoom in again. Among those seventeen students is one girl. Focus on the one blonde girl standing in the center. See the blonde girl, who tried something new at the onset of her senior year. Her name is Stephanie. There are some moments that stay with you forever. Time can pass yet the influence of one person can be engraved on your soul. I still call these seventeen team members my kids.

Four years later, on October 17, 2009, I was standing in the kitchen when I heard my phone ring. I answered to the near whispers on the other end.

"Karen, has anyone called you?" She paused. "Have you heard?" asked Megan, one of my kids. Her voice cracked. My entire body froze. I felt the blood drain from my face before she could whisper anything more.

"It's Stephanie. She was in a car accident. She didn't make it."

I couldn't breathe. It felt like someone was trying to constrict my heart, crush my lungs. Certainly it had to be a mistake.

But it wasn't. I lost one of my kids.

There are billions of people in the world, five thousand people can fill an arena, seventeen students can stand together in a room, and still, that one girl matters. My heart still hurts. One person, the one person, really does have value.

There is a scrapbook with a personal note and a picture from each of the seventeen team members. You can see a smiling face and read words like, "I can't express with words how much this year has meant to me." You can look at each individual picture, each individual person, and recognize worth.

Stephanie didn't suddenly become valuable to us because of tragedy. She has been important, significant, and valuable all along. That one girl matters, and so do you.

Have you ever felt insignificant? Have you ever wondered if you really matter? We live on a planet full of billions of people. Millions live on our continent, thousands of people in our cities. There are hundreds of people walking around in our schools. There are people in our neighborhoods and people at work. We are surrounded by beautiful people, talented people, and people who we think live exciting lives.

Please, know that you matter.

Sometimes we feel lost. Instead of understanding the significance of the one, we get distracted by the seventeen, the forty, or the five thousand. With all the feelings of competition and clamor, it is easy to feel misplaced, forgotten, and insignificant.

Please, know that you matter.

There are times we see achievements, educational degrees, high end fashion, or popularity and we feel less than. There are times we get defensive when we talk about soccer players versus cheerleaders, stay-at-home versus working moms, or corporate executives versus mail room staff. There are times we rank one another. There are times we pick teams, we name one group better than another, and we start creating a hierarchy. But the truth of it is that all people have value.

Please, know that you matter.

You are not insignificant. You have experiences no one else has. You have a unique fingerprint. You have a heartbeat. You breathe, you feel. You have a unique perspective. You could tell your own story of struggle and joy. There are lives you probably don't even know that you are impacting.

Please, know that you matter.

There are moments where we look at the people that surround us and we feel inferior, we may think we are minimized, or we even may wonder why one person magically has it all together while we are stuck. We may wonder, "When will it be my turn?"

Please, I plead with you, you need to understand how much you matter.

Understanding self-worth will make you free. You will not need to worry, "What will people think?" You will not need to ask, "Do I look okay?" You will not be looking around for approval because you will powerfully be able to generate your own. Having knowledge and a conviction of your worth will help you move forward with influence and peace.

Becoming emotionally centered

Many people get caught up in the billions of people that are on the planet and feel trivial and lost. It's easy to discredit ourselves.

When you see someone else in a successful career, you still matter. When you see an attractive person, you are still important. When you see your neighbor's home, talents, or family, know there are still no conditions to your own worth.

I first started researching self-worth in college as part of a capstone thesis project and since then have spent ten years paying attention. I've been humbled to read the responses of hundreds of teenagers who shared their most intense pressures. My heart has ached for the thousands of women who have let me glimpse their battle with depression. I've been watching and listening to people like you, trying to make sense of this struggle.

6

I'm not exempt. I feel the struggle. I understand what it's like to battle the emotional roller coaster. I've sat through a class and missed out on learning because I was convinced the beautiful, talented instructor minimized me. I've stayed awake until two o'clock in the morning analyzing my conversations. "Why did I say that? What are they going to think?"

I've had days I didn't want to get out of bed. I fear failure. I've felt discouragement because of how my jeans fit. I understand what it's like to question my importance as a person.

But I also know I must be constantly vigilant. I've learned what to do when the pressure hits so I can function as a wife and mother. I've studied how to handle emotions of inadequacy. When I'm in the same room as hundreds of people, and see that perceived perfect person, I've learned the thought process and skills I need so I don't walk away feeling worthless.

No one can escape emotions of inadequacy. But we can all learn how to become emotionally centered. I've learned the more emotionally centered I am, the more I can see and celebrate others, sincerely, without feeling like they're a threat.

There have been late nights going through surveys and long afternoons spent in the junior high after-school program. There have been post-conference conversations with a tearful mother, a confused teen, a youth leader. I've heard it expressed from the professional counselor, the concerned father, the single woman, the school teacher, and many others like you. There are phrases I hear repeated frequently.

"I'm hard on myself."

"I'm not happy when I look in the mirror."

"I will never be good enough."

"People are judging me."

"I'm not at peace."

"I don't feel good about myself."

"I wish I knew how to change it."

It's widespread. We're losing courage. We feel uncertain. Inadequacy and depression are consuming our culture. We're weak, exhausted. This is not a little problem that's going to go away with time. This battle is raging in every community, every high school, every family, and every home. Stop and see it. It's there. We don't need statistics, simply think about the people in your life.

You've witnessed it. You've experienced it.

Words we think and say have serious emotional consequences. We expect a lot out of ourselves. We constantly try to hide, conceal, and alter things we don't like about our appearance. We criticize our body. We feel minimized, put down, and diminished to the point we cannot function. We may live in fear, constantly trying to please, impress, hide from, or control what others think as a way to deal with our insecurity

One woman I met said, "I'm miserable! I'm at war with myself, but I don't even know what I can do about it." A teenager uttered the phrase, "I'm a nobody." Another person shared, "I'm stuck. I wish I knew what it takes to be confident."

What is self-worth?

We have a hard time knowing what we can do to stop feeling so worthless. Many of our problems can be worked out if we understand self-worth. You can develop skills and learn techniques. You can live peacefully, on purpose. Self-worth is quite simple. There is one place you need to start. You must first develop the basic understanding of what self-worth is. Then live in harmony with that definition. Don't make it complex.

Self-worth is your constant value. Your worth is always there. It does not change. There is something significant about being a person. You automatically have meaning. No conditions. You matter. The one person is important.

Self-worth is not something you must earn. It's something you must recognize. We are often wrong about what self-worth means. We confuse identity and self-worth as something we produce. So much emotional pain could be healed if we could comprehend there is nothing that we need to prove. There are no requirements.

You will not need to say, "I will matter if . . ." or use the phrase, "I matter because . . ." as a way to demonstrate your significance. It is not about the things we should do. It is not necessary to prove anything because self-worth is already established. Rather, it's about simply using the words "I matter."

We misunderstand self-worth if we think that it is something that can be changed, bought, altered, or manipulated. We misunderstand self-worth when we think it changes. The correct definition of self-worth is genuine, infinite, and complete. Understanding self-worth means we live to recognize unconditional value.

We all have struggles. We each receive messages. Everyone has a story.

Meet a woman we'll call Julia. Her curly blonde hair frames her trim cheekbones and green eyes. Julia can still tell you the name of the ninth grade boy that called her names and made fun of her zits. She went through high school feeling invisible, alone, and like her self-esteem had been shattered. She cried a lot. Anytime someone would give her a compliment, she would disregard it, question it.

People have shared, "I never feel smart enough." They've said, "I'm consumed by depression and inadequacy. I'll never be someone worth taking a second look at." We may feel pressure to please, worry about the opinions of others, and have a hard time feeling what we have to say is important. We are lost, overwhelmed, and confused.

What is your story? Life seems to be filled with unmet expectations, uncontrollable thoughts, hurt, and insignificance. We may have memories of others who've made fun of us. Many can recall the exact moment another person took away our feelings of worth. It can consume us with grief, hurt the people we love, and prevent us from reaching our full potential.

Forgiveness and a fresh start

One woman held on to her story of loss. She allowed

the pain that happened years ago to be as raw today as the day it happened. Constantly focusing on her loss, she developed a pattern of suppressing her own strength. She relied on everyone else, to an unhealthy degree, to tell her she had value. She needed sympathy, compliments, attention, and constant approval from others. In fact she thrived on it. She would use her story over and over again as a short-term-ever-changing-never-reliable-for-long way to get the acceptance she was desperately looking for.

Why would you let something painful continue to run your life?

It may be because we don't know any different, we've been conditioned to think and live like that, or because we fear future hurt.

People who rely on the strength of others tend to disregard compliments, apologize beyond courtesy, manipulate, seek affirmation, use uncomfortable sarcasm, or dwell on negativity. Those who refuse to see their own strength seem to be exhausted, disappointed, and hurt time and time again. People may say things like, "But I was abused. . . ." Other people will say, "You just don't understand how hard life has been for me. . . ."

"The ninth grade boy that called me names still mocks me. All these years later, I can still hear his voice when I look in the mirror."

"I grew up in poverty. The dress I never owned still haunts me."

"My sister was the beautiful one. Everyone told her she was pretty. No one said that to me. To this day I don't, nor will I ever, believe I am pretty."

The loss you suffered, the divorce that shattered your family, the messages you have heard, these are hard things. But don't let them become your foundation. Shame, embarrassment, and hurt should not guide our lives.

It's a very defensive way to live. Too many people search for peace by wallowing in their own pain. Let go. You don't need to forget everything, because it is good to remember the experiences that make you who you are. But stop protecting yourself with pain.

There are times we let the most hurtful aspects of our lives act as a shield that prevents anything good from coming. There are times we fend off help, run from, and fear the things that will help us most. It's time to forgive. Sometimes you have to forgive another person, and sometimes you have to forgive yourself. As you heal you will be able to feel a stronger sense of acceptance and peace. You must be willing to try. You must pay attention to how you've conditioned yourself to think. You must have the courage to reach your potential. It's time for a fresh start.

Instead of starting with the foundations of what self-worth means, we tend to want to start with all the complicated matters. We want to use the word *but* to justify just how trivial our struggles have made us. Life can be very difficult. It is in these moments of real raw emotion that self-worth looks complicated.

Yes, heritage and genetics can impact how we see ourselves. Yes, life is hard. Yes, depression is real.

Yes, there are circumstances that can prevent us from seeing how great we are. Abuse, loss, discouragement, divorce, childhood trauma, disappointment, feelings of failure, and messages we've received can be wounds that distance us from understanding self-worth. Before struggle, amid struggle, and after struggle, you must find out for yourself that you still have individual worth.

The difference between self-worth and self-esteem

If self-worth is your unconditional value, then self-esteem can be defined as your perception of worth. Your view is what changes. Your worth does not.

Think about a weight-loss advertisement. The person featured in a glamorous "after" setting expresses with a smile, "Now I have my self-esteem back." It's the idea that self-esteem is something you have or you don't. It's the idea that the higher your self-esteem, the higher your happiness and success. So we do anything we can to find this elusive self-esteem.

Self-esteem refers to the level of value you feel. Think about the words *high self-esteem* and *low self-esteem*. You're a good person. You're a bad person. You believe in yourself. You doubt yourself. You're skinny. You're fat. You're on trend. You're out of date. You're popular. You're a nobody. You're on top. You're scum, secondary, the low man on the totem pole. How are you evaluating your worth? What is the opinion you have about yourself?

We get overwhelmed trying to find high self-esteem, upset when it leaves us, and confused when we feel change. We've been conditioned to categorize and rate our worth. Seeking high self-esteem can set you up for failure. It's limited by the natural tendencies of your mind.

Think about the highs, lows, changes, dips, dives, and conditions. Consider all the scrambling, competing, clawing, attempting, withdrawing, and perfection-based vying we go through to tell people how much we matter. Constantly proving, ever justifying that we're good enough. Isn't it exhausting?

Feelings of low self-esteem can be very real and debilitating. Self-esteem implies competition, rank, change, rivalry, and position. Self-esteem is based on hierarchy. It's complicated. High self-esteem implies it has to be earned and maintained. There is no long-term peace with self-esteem, even if it is high self-esteem, because you will always be limited to your perceived success and failures.

Self-esteem is fickle and uncertain while self-worth is steady and reliable. See the difference.   Self-esteem changes where self-worth is constant. Self-worth, as it's truly unconditional, is not a struggle, it's instantly obtainable, and it's clear. Self-worth is continuous. You do not need to compete to have self-worth. Self-worth can take into account the slip ups and imperfections that come from just being a person. It's simple, you matter.

What language should you use?

There are times we get confused on what wording we should actually use: *self-worth* or *self-esteem*?

Whenever possible, consider making self-worth your word of choice. Emphasizing the word *self-worth* in your vocabulary will highlight the idea that you already matter. You don't have to compete for value. We already get bombarded with better-than-less-than messages and using the word *self-worth* helps us to let go of the unnecessary competition.

Although it is appropriate to use the word *self-esteem* when we are referencing the highs and lows of how we feel about self, we need to be aware that self-esteem is not self-worth. Consider letting go of the battle for high self-esteem and instead find out what having self-worth allows you to experience.

The benefits of understanding self-worth

Understanding self-worth will impact every aspect of your life. If you're focused on a low self-esteem, it will impact what you think, feel, and do. It will impact your relationships. It will influence how frantic you are over the opinions of other people. It will impact your future, your goals, and your ability to reach your potential. Consider how you treat others and how they treat you, how you show love, how you allow others to show love to you. Misunderstanding self-worth leads to fear, discouragement, and depression.

If you don't understand self-worth you may become critical of others, make assumptions, become overly sensitive, settle for less, or hold back. You may refuse the kindness of a loved one. You may look in the mirror and physically ache. You may feel shame, embarrassment, discouragement, or anger. These barriers can cause hearts to hurt, opportunities to be lost, and conflict in relationships.

We've been condition to rank people. We have an instinct to protect ourselves through competition. We often assume that another person's success means that we are a failure. People play games, manipulate, tear others down, scramble, sugar coat, sabotage, blame, conceal, criticize, betray, bully, or display indirect hostility all in a quest for success. They don't truly understand self-worth.

What's getting in your way from seeing that you already matter?

If you understand self-worth you are more likely to be resilient through struggle, cultivate powerful relationships, celebrate the success of others, and live a healthy life. People who feel a sense of unconditional value are less likely to engage in gossip, less likely to bully, less likely to be resentful, less likely to feel defensive, and less likely to demean others.

Those who understand self-worth tend to treat people with respect and kindness. They can take risks with less fear, feel empowered to make decisions, reach goals, and can better explore elements outside of their comfort zone. Understanding self-worth allows you to experience love more powerfully. Overall, understanding self-worth is one of the most powerful indicators of feeling happiness and success.

Self-worth is unconditional. Do you understand what this means for you? If you can see and allow this to take root in your life you will be able to find a stronger sense of peace, confidence, and live life more fully.

Self-Worth is your constant value. Your worth is always there. It does not change. There is something significant about being a person. You automatically have meaning. No conditions.

Self-Esteem is your perception of your worth. Even though you are already important, your ability to see your unconditional value is the aspect that changes. Self-esteem is always shifting.

Self-Acceptance is the continual process of learning about our identity, striving for contentment, and recognizing weaknesses without resenting them.

Potential is what you can become.

Confidence is faith in ability. It doesn't mean you have a perfect knowledge of success. It does mean that you understand yourself enough to take action.

Knowing who you are is process.
Don't feel like you have to know
every little thing about yourself
today. Allow this definition to be
flexible. Learn about yourself,
pay attention,
and then adjust.

Chapter 2

I Know Who I Am

Remember who you are.

What does that even mean? My parents would often say those words when I left the house as a teenager. Remember? Come on, Mom, like I'm going to forget my name.

Picture a twelve-year-old girl who throws her hands in the air and out of desperation cries, "I don't even know who I am." Consider what happens to a star high school football player after he no longer has an opportunity to play football. There is also the young mother who just welcomed an identity crisis along with the beautiful new baby. Why might a forty-year-old say, "I am a lot more at peace with my life now than when I was in my twenties, because I know who I am now"? Why might a fifty-year-old go through a mid-life crisis? Think about a grandmother who sits in her quiet home, wondering what value her life has now that no one is at around to enjoy her home-cooked meals. Identity impacts everyone.

The Haley Myth

To understand this better, let me take you back to my freshman year of high school. At age fourteen, in northern Louisiana, I felt a cresting pressure to "be someone." I had built up the idea that if I was going to be someone who was important I needed to be pretty, well-liked, participate in the right activities, and know the right people.

I remember looking at a gorgeous, popular, brunette girl with perfect hair. Her name was Haley, and I thought, "Wow, she is so lucky to be *the* important girl." She sat at the right bench. She ate lunch with the cool kids. She knew the right people. She wore the right clothes. She was talented and involved in the right extracurricular activities. She was smart and everyone thought she was beautiful. I adored Haley. I mentally built Haley up to be perfect, valued by all of Airline High School, and magically bestowed with the gift of confidence and "high self-esteem." She must have known all the secrets. She must have this perfect knowledge of who she is. How would it be to be her, someone beautiful, talented, and confident with a great pair of shoes? I thought she had no struggles.

The truth was, as I got to know Haley, I recognized she was a person. She had insecurities. She didn't consider herself to be born with the confidence gene. She wasn't perfect, but she was a good person who was making good decisions. The more I got to know Haley, the more I saw how all people struggle with insecurities. There is power in understanding another person's life. You can see that no one is exempt from struggle. There are no perfect people living perfect lives.

The truth about self-worth is that confidence is not

an unexplainable thing that just magically happens to a lucky few people. Confidence is not about having a perfect knowledge. Individual worth encompasses principles of choice, accountability, and daily effort.

We create ourselves. We aren't just thrown into a room full of people hoping we get the luck of the important-person draw. We ultimately choose who we are. I love this principle because it erases what we can call the "Haley Myth," which is the idea that we are either born with self-worth or we are stuck. It dispels the idea that some people instantly experience assurance, and some people don't.

It focuses, rather, on a lifetime decision-making process instead of the perception that another person is lucky. It's easy to assume others don't struggle. All people have challenges. We will each experience a sense of confusion and curiosity about identity to some degree.

Three misconceptions about identity

Be assured that there is choice in confidence. The first myth is that we are stuck. We can't do anything about our identity, we were born with a specific set of traits, and we are limited. Even though we may naturally have a specific disposition or character trait, we still have the power to choose. We have the capability to decide who we want to be and we can act for ourselves. We are not stuck. Confidence is explainable as it involves the ability to become and believe.

Another misconception about self-worth is we are insignificant because of our circumstances. Some circumstances are heartbreaking and difficult. I'm so sorry if you are going through something painful. Struggle is real. It hurts. These situations can be the barriers that prevent us from feeling like we matter. But please understand, no matter what circumstances have been placed in your life, you are not insignificant.

Difficult situations do not make you inferior. Circumstances that you do not like do not make you worthless. Pain that others have caused for you does not mean you matter less.

A third area where we get confused is when we think that identity is a one-time event. Being able to say, "I know who I am," will just one day click and stay constant the rest of your life is incorrect. Knowing who you are is a process that will change and need to be evaluated all through our lives. From the moment we are born until we take our last breath, we make decisions and have experiences that ultimately determine who we are.

You will not one day wake up and find yourself. There may be a day after consistent effort you will notice you feel more at peace. But you must recognize that just because you know who you are one moment, doesn't mean that that picture you painted in your mind is going to be the same ten years from now. It sets us up for disappointment, confusion, and future hurt when we don't allow identity to change.

Feeling lost

"I've got to find myself" is another phrase we commonly use. It implies that we are feeling lost, that we are trying to figure ourselves out, that one day it might all just click.

In order to find themselves some people may take special soul-searching pilgrimages to exotic places like Peru. Teenagers experiment with popular catch phrases like, "totally." Men buy sports cars. Women get a makeover. This can all be in an attempt to discover what about life can explain us.

Have you experienced confusing identity moments in life? Have you ever felt lost? Experiences might vary from person to person, but we are all going to go through a process of change and adjustment.

After I had my third child, I was pacing the house at two in the morning exhausted. I wondered, "What happened to my life?" So much had changed. I went from doing community outreach programs to lonely nights soothing a crying child. "Who am I?"

"What's happened to me?"

Having a baby jar me awake with constant crying, not being able to even have a conversation with my husband, watching the dishes pile up because my arms were otherwise occupied was enough cause to question myself. Every time I have had one of my children, I have had to adjust the ideas, themes, and concepts I associate with myself. This is only one example.

When have you experienced identity questions?

I've personally had identity questions as a teenager figuring out friends, extracurricular activities, and dating. But it's not just for teens. I've questioned who I was when I graduated high school, when I left home, when I decided on a college major, when I got married, when my grandma passed away, when I moved, when I took a job, when I quit a job, and when my oldest child went to kindergarten for the first time. This is only a sample list. We are constantly making decisions about our identity.

I expect these identity questions to continue my entire life and I'm at peace with that. It may sound discouraging. Life is a never-ending identity crisis? Instead of seeing this change as a crisis, we can embrace it with excitement and hope for the future. The more we understand what goes into it, the better off we can be. Our entire life becomes an opportunity to craft who we want to be.

Break it down: Who are you?

When my daughter was four-years-old, I would express words of love to her. One day she stopped, looked me in the eye, and said, "Why? Why do you love me, Mommy?"

I was surprised by her question. I truly had to think about it, I love her, but I had no idea how to put it into words. I often repeat the phrase to her, "I love you always, forever, no matter what. You are my baby."

As she continued to ask why I loved her, I recognized that even though unconditional love is at the foundation of self-worth, we still cling to words that help us understand who we are. It's a need. We should and must discover the clarity and details of our complete makeup.

Even though I had no conditions to the love for my daughter, I started to naturally share more information with her so she could understand who she is and feel a sense of comfort.

"I love you because you are kind. Thank you for sharing your toys."

"I love you because you are happy. When you skip, it makes me smile. You fill our home with joy."

"I love you because you are good. I appreciate that you listen to me and Daddy."

"I love you because you are beautiful. I look in your eyes, run my fingers through your hair, and I think you're pretty."

"I love you because you are smart. You're doing great with your ABCs."

Over time I continued to recognize why I did love her and why she was a person of value. I love her for who she is and what she can become.

Who she is? Who are you?

Don't make it complex. Remember, we try to make self-worth much more difficult than it needs to be. Keep it basic. We've already established self-worth is unconditional. Next, learn with clarity and details the nature of your identity. This can bring you confidence.

Identity is a word we use a lot, but seldom can we describe what it means. Simply put, identity is what a person is. It includes our complete makeup.

Knowing who you are can be divided into four concepts. This is called the Identity Grid. Anytime we use the words "I know who I am" or "identity," we are referring to the framework of four categories: heritage, values, traits, and choices.

The Identity Grid
1. Heritage: Where do you come from?

The foundation of your identity starts with your ancestry and is built upon by experience.

No matter if you are proud of your heritage or if you have a past full of hurt, we wouldn't be where we are today without the people and events that came before us. Heritage is foundational and it impacts our decisions. This can include how you were raised, where you were raised, your religion, your grandparent's identity (remember identity means heritage, values, traits, and choice), your parent's identity, where you've lived, where your family is from, and what you've experienced up to this point. What are your genetics, family histories, and biology?

Each person is susceptible to the elements we have been exposed to and the memories we have experienced both good and bad. Discover the clarity and details of your heritage. As you read the examples think about your life and try to put it into your own words. *"I come from . . ."*

I am Emily. I come from a blended family. I was born in California. I am Cherie's granddaughter.

Have you ever met a family deeply rooted in tradition? Think about a family that lives and loves the same small town, generation after generation. Consider a military family who's had the opportunity to live in many different locations. Think about that child that comes from a proud Italian family, Polynesian family, or Hispanic family.

Consider traditions like Sunday dinner, going to football games together, eating blueberry pancakes on Saturday morning, or meeting at the baseball field for fireworks every Fourth of July. There is the single-mother family, the family with step-parents, the family with an only child, or the family of all boys. Think about the experiences they've had and how it impacts the makeup of one person.

Consider a foundational heritage of love of country, belief that you are a child of God, hard work to build a home, the sacrifice of grandpa during the Great Depression, the dad who never had the opportunity to go to college, or strength of grandma during adversity and how that shapes us as individuals.

I met a teen who was in the foster care system. Her biological mother struggled with drug abuse, her father was in prison, she was bounced around from foster home to foster home, and she was in the process of legally living on her own at age sixteen. This is part of her heritage. This impacts who she is. Her heritage is foundational and it impacts other aspects of identity.

Even though this teen has experienced a difficult sixteen years of life and has what many people would call an unstable foundation—a heritage you probably want to run from—it was very inspiring to see this girl take strength from her past and use it to shape her future.

She focused on what she wanted to become. She focused on what she experienced and how, because of that, she wanted to make a better life.

One of the most exciting things to discover about identity is that even though heritage is typically out of our control, we decide how we let it impact our future. No matter if it is an inspiring foundation laced with example or an uneven foundation that has stories of struggle and hurt, we choose how to respond.

I have grandparents and parents who've deeply influence my own life. I feel like everything that is good in my life can be traced back to the perseverance, patience, and love set by the people that come before me.

What is your heritage like?

My grandpa served in the military and often gave us jelly beans. When I see an American flag, I feel gratitude, I feel loved, and I think about jelly beans.

My mom moved around a lot, being in a military family, and I moved a lot as a child due to my dad's job changes. Because I grew up with change, I like to rearrange furniture. Because I didn't grow up with the same friends I had from kindergarten, I notice today how this impacts my friendships. I tend to keep people at a distance. I fear losing dear friendships, and it's hard for me to let people in. It's one of my examples of using hurt to protect myself.

What about you?

There are elements about my childhood I absolutely cherish and take strength from. Yet there are also elements that lead me to make different decisions. Even though heritage shapes us, ultimately we decide how we let it impact our future.

For example, growing up I remember my parents encouraged our family to be thrifty and make do with clothing and shoes. I remember being allowed only two pair of shoes, one for everyday and a nice pair for church. There were moments I felt like saying, "Please, what about dress boots, high tops, and strappy sandals?" There were days I thought, "I can't wear a brown belt with black shoes." I would watch my friends have sporty shoes, sparkly shoes, and tall shoes. Still, the family approach on shoes was one of simplicity.

Those memories impact me today. I love shoes. As an adult, I love going to my closet and saying, "I choose you, blue suede ballet flats." I love holding new pair of black heels and just smelling them.

It is not resentful or with lack of respect to my heritage. I'm still mindful of the lesson on frugality that was taught to me. I can still honor and use the lessons on simplicity. I'm grateful to my parents. But the way I purchase and wear shoes is different than what I did in my childhood.

We learn from our heritage, we grow from it, we take strength from it. Our experiences and our heritage help to explain who we are.

2. Values: What do you believe in?

Values are an important part of our identity. Values are our standards of behavior. They shape and highlight how we strive to live and what our priorities are. We can't stand for something if we don't know what we value.

You'll find after reviewing heritage, many of our values come from the things we did or did not experience in our past. Values are our code of conduct, and they highlight how we should live. You can put anything in this category that will complete the phrase, "*I believe in.*"

I believe in hard work and spending less than I earn. I believe in family and I believe in God. Trust is important to me. I believe in taking time to be adventurous like going for hikes and taking last-minute vacations.

You can start thinking about traits like honesty, generosity, health, spirituality, knowledge, community, or loyalty. Do any of these beliefs resonate with you?

Consider family and relationships. We may believe in love, kindness, respect, home, and spending time together. There are values associated with faith like virtue, holiness, hope, good works, devotion, grace, balance, or mercy.

Reflect on career, education, or ambitions. Sometimes we hold tight to control, order, accountability, dependability, accuracy, or accomplishment. It may be important to be punctual, professional, or powerful.

Don't disregard creativity. Do you believe in innovation, design, or authenticity? What about your entertainment? There are beliefs associated with spontaneity, relationships, fun, and how leisure time should be spent. Friendships impact what we believe in. How do you feel about gossip, kindness, sensitivity, integrity, and optimism?

Values are at the core of peace and happiness. Many of our internal battles can be explained by how we match our behavior with our values. A great sense of confusion comes when we are unclear on what our values are. If you are feeling lost or experiencing a sense of identity confusion, the first category you should review is values. Are you living in line with what you believe? When behavior matches values, we tend to feel at peace. When we act differently than what we believe, we feel conflict.

A lack of confidence can often be traced to faltering or dishonored values. Our values are a powerful, and often overlooked, component to feeling confidence. You've got to know what you believe in.

I remember waiting at the middle school bus stop one cold morning while a neighborhood girl was being teased. While standing by the curbside, a group of three boys started making fun of her naturally curly hair. They called her names.

I looked down. I didn't make eye contact. It was too uncomfortable to stand up for her. She stood alone for five minutes while I pretended not to notice. Not only do I vividly remember the pain of a person being made fun of, I still feel the conflict that comes from not living in line with what I believe. I didn't honor my values. It made me sick.

When we do not make decisions that support our beliefs, we dishonor our core identity and that causes tension. If you are not at peace with yourself, it is crucial to both understand what you value, then you must live those values.

My values were put to the test in another situation in response to one of my life-long dreams. I love laughter, and for years I pictured myself doing stand-up comedy. I've always been known as the self-worth girl, but silently I've been writing jokes on the side. I kept a pile of notebooks for five years on funny observations before I ever got the courage to do something with it.

With a joyful terror, I finally researched comedy clubs, wrote a set, contacted the club, and made the hour long drive. I was going to live my dream. As I checked in, I experienced anxiety equivalent to trying to squish a spider, while going to the dentist, while singing the national anthem in a sold-out sports arena. But this was something I really wanted to do.

As I was gearing up to deliver my set, I started to hear words, language, and expressions from the other comedians that physically hurt my already unsettled stomach. I know humor means different things to different people, but the standard in the comedy club included extremes in subjects I consider sacred, with crude descriptions designated to shock the audience into laughter. It was like watching a shoddy rap music video with an advisory label, and I couldn't hit the pause button. I tried to tune out the hard language, and I did my set. I should have been relieved and excited as I just accomplish a goal years in the making, but I felt so unsettled.

Afterward, the evening emcee told me I could do this. Another comedian told me my writing was good.

"Come back," they said.

I had an opportunity to pursue my dream. Did it mean I would jeopardize my values? I am a mother. What would my children say about the comedy club versus our home? I wasn't the one who was delivering the crude jokes. Couldn't I just tune it out? This felt like my only location option. I was accomplishing something I sincerely wanted to do. It was the best place to hone my technique. Think of the opportunity I could have performing here. People would think I was prude for letting it go.

Let go of my dream or change my standards, that's what it came down to. I knew the behavior at the comedy club was not consistent with what I would allow in my home. I knew my true identity, my core beliefs.

I made the decision to not go back to the comedy club. I felt discouraged. It was the harder road. Yet I knew it was in line with who I am. I would have always felt unsettled there, because I would not be honoring my identity. It took more effort to find locations where I could try new material, yet I feel strength for making a decision that honored my values. Especially in that it was a hard decision. I don't need to worry about what things I will see and hear that may influence how I lead my children or audiences. I still live my comedy dream but I choose to take a different path.

What we believe in and how we behave in line with those beliefs impact our sense of peace. If I believe in health and importance of my body and I exercise and eat right, I am more likely to feel right. If I believe in health and I believe in the joy of ice cream, well, then I may experience conflict. Ultimately one belief will be of greater priority. Sometimes the ice cream wins.

Values can and do change. When I was in college, I valued spontaneity, freedom, and adventure. Now I value structure, being at home, and security. Are there times in your life standards of behavior changed?

Sometimes that lost "I don't know who I am" plea comes from not truly knowing what we believe in, what we live for, and what we live by. Learn to define your values by recognizing times in your life you were happy, and the behaviors and priorities associated with that.

3. Traits: Performance, personality, and physical.

We can break down traits into three categories to understand them even better.

Performance traits: What do you do?

What is your role? What positions do you hold? What are your daily responsibilities? A powerful aspect of who you are comes down to your daily tasks.

Think about the duties, the assignments, the profession, or the role you presently have. Performance traits change the most frequently and can cause us to wonder who we are every time we make a decision or make a change concerning what we do with our life. Answer this by creating a list of what you do.

I am a college student, I am studying biology, and I work as a CNA in a nursing home.

I am a mother, I am a friend, I play soccer, and I teach an aerobics class.

I am a husband, I am a realtor, I run marathons, and I enjoy working in the yard on the weekends.

Personality traits: What are you like?

This includes your strengths, temperament, tendencies, quirks, fears, passions, and favorites. Knowing little things like your likes, dislikes, hopes, fears, and dreams can help you begin to build confidence. What words describe you?

Personality traits can usually be the most difficult to see and can be the hardest to put into words.

I am reserved, I tend to be shy, and I'm good with numbers. I like to listen to people, so when I'm in a group I usually don't talk. I love how getting up early in the morning makes my mind clear; it's the best time to think and plan for the future.

I am happy, optimistic. I have high energy. I love singing in the shower and I'm afraid of failure. I'm passionate about animals and I love puppies.

I am good at negotiating. I am quiet but strong. I like to eat peanut butter on apples. I am passionate about rock music.

Our personality impacts how we view life. It is the characteristics we have when we interact with people, interpret life, and make decisions. The distinct way we think and act, whether it's outgoing or reserved, is part of our makeup. We may like to focus on the details or we may rather focus on people.

Personality traits can be impacted by our heritage, experience, and environments. Birth order, for example, impacts what we are like. My oldest son has had more expectations, more attention, and more new-parent-excitement put on him than our third child. We were potty training at two, where baby number three may be wearing diapers in kindergarten. Parents can get tired and busy. The oldest child may enjoy being in charge or feel a need to please more than the youngest child.

These describing traits are attributes of our thoughts, behaviors, and actions. Consider people who are helpful, kind, and encouraging. Some people are imaginative, artistic, or creative. Some people may be meticulous, observant, fair, and thoughtful. Others may be fearless, dependable, bold, and are good being in charge.

Learn what your strengths and weaknesses are. Learn what environments make you thrive. Put your passions into words. What's your temperament? What makes you weird, awesome, and an individual? Describe your favorites. Try to get a feel for your personality.

Physical traits: What do you look like?

Like it or not, what you look like is part of who you are. We are more than just a body, yes. But your body in its current state is part of who you are. It plays a major impact on your outlook.

Take some time to think about what you look like without tearing your appearance down. Don't record your physical traits with hostility. Stay neutral as you answer the question "What do you look like?" Keep your dissatisfaction out of it.

I have short brown hair and blue eyes. I'm five foot eight inches tall. I am curvy. I have my mom's dimples. I wear a size nine shoe. I have a scar from a car accident.

36

I have long straight hair that is light in color. I have brown eyes and round cheekbones. I'm short. I have strong legs. I have stretch marks.

The mistakes we make with traits

After reviewing these three aspects of our traits, performance, personality, and physical, you are better prepared to understand the mistakes we make. We make the biggest identity mistakes in this category. Usually it's because we forget about every other category and think we are exclusively our traits. When we only use performance, personality, or physical traits to define who we are, we're at risk for confusion, heartache, depression, feelings of loss, and having a hard time dealing with change.

Think about what you do—your performance traits. If you were a star basketball player throughout high school, what happens when you get an injury, don't make the college team, or can't play competitive basketball anymore? Your identity takes a hit.

Think about the question, "What do you do?" Many stay-at-home moms go through identity battles because motherhood becomes the only framework of who you are. If you spend years focusing on the demands of motherhood without exploring any other aspect of your identity, you set yourself up for identity confusion. You may feel neglected and empty. A time will come when the kids won't need you quite the same anymore, and again, life may feel pointless and empty.

Performance can easily become the only gauge

of who you are. A person can get so focused on their personality that they can disregard their heritage. It's easy to let only your body define your identity.

What do you look like? When you base who you are on appearance, you are limited to the success or failure of your appearance. If you are known for your long hair or flawless complexion, what happens if you get your hair cut or get a zit? You get an identity crisis.

Understanding the Identity Grid can help you through times like these. When you struggle with your traits you can take strength from another area like heritage, values, or choice.

Traits change

In his early twenties, my husband, Cory, was a water-skier, he was a college student, and he was bold, clever, and fun. When I first met my husband, he had striking hair. Fast forward ten years and see how these traits can adjust. Cory now sports a shaved head to better accommodate his bald spot. Although he still has a love for water skiing, it probably wouldn't be top of the daily to-do list. My husband's disposition is still full of fun, but we now see how three kids and a career in marriage and family therapy has adjusted his personality traits and tendencies.

Recognize that your traits are going to change and need to be evaluated all throughout life.

4. Choices: What do you want to be?

The most powerful, and perhaps the most important,

aspect of our identity involves choices. No matter what traits we have, or what our heritage is, we ultimately decide the person we want to be. We can act for ourselves.

Responsibility and accountability play a vital role in identity. We are in charge of the decisions we make. How accountable we are directly impacts how confident we feel. You have control over who you are today and who you want to become.

Just because we want to be President of the United States, a professional baseball player, or a world famous musician doesn't mean that we can suddenly become those people. Rather we choose the daily attitudes that can help us reach our potential. Dream and live to be your ideal self.

What do you want to be?

I want to be kind. I want to be known as the person who sees and support others. I want to be happy.

I want to travel and be adventurous, so I've saved my money and planned my first trip.

I want to create a home where people want to gather. I want to be known as a welcoming person.

I want to wake up earlier and get to school on time.

Have you ever met someone you instantly felt inspired by and wanted to know? When I first met Jeni Roper, I was filled with admiration. I really wanted to know who she was. Jeni stands with a smile, a spunky hair cut, and she wiggles. You see, Jeni has cerebral palsy, a condition that causes her body to shake. Her wiggle, to some people, would be a physical trait you think would define her and limit her opportunities. But Jeni chooses to go for her dreams. Jeni acts.

I watched Jeni stand on a stage, with the microphone shaking in her hands, and receive a standing ovation for her ability to be herself. She is a person who will stand in a room full of people and say exactly what she is thinking. She is an inspiration, a great speaker. It's powerful to see Jenni pursue who she wants to become. Jeni is someone who utilizes the power of choice in identity.

We are often drawn to people who exemplify the power of choice—who decide who they want to be. What do you want in your life? What are you becoming?

Your potential is part of who you are. Perhaps one of the most inspiring aspects is seeing beyond all the elements you have right now and recognizing what you are capable of. Each of us has the ability to grow. Sometimes we've got to reach deep in order to see what we have the ability to do. There may be qualities you don't have, yet if you want them, they can still be a part of your identity. There is power in exploring what you desire out of life.

Identity is imperfect and changing

Identity is an imperfect knowledge. It is always changing. It will need to be evaluated, and reevaluated all throughout your life. What is true about your heritage, values, traits, and choice when you are twenty is going to be different than when you are forty. Even though your heritage is quite stable, you will be able to add new concepts of where you have been. You may find your values become more concrete and find that some standards of behavior need updating. You may see changes in your traits, not only does your body age, but your favorites change, and the answer to what you do will be different. Even though there are core personality traits that will be consistent, you will be making choices your entire life.

Knowing who you are is a process. Don't feel like you have to know every little thing about yourself today. Allow this definition to be flexible. Learn about yourself, pay attention, and then adjust. You can say "I know who I am" and recognize that this information can change.

Expressing individuality

We all have a desire to show people who we are. Some people make a bold, loud stand such as wearing clothing with animal print, sharing political views, or talking loudly in a crowd. Other people express an identifying mark using quiet or subliminal ways. Individuality is setting yourself apart, showing what makes you distinguishable, or emphasizing concepts that describe who you are.

My trademark smell is vanilla. I love basic vanilla candles, soaps, and I even add extra vanilla extract to my cookies. My husband knows he can get me creamy vanilla lotion as a gift, and it will be a hit.

Have you noticed the struggle to be distinguishable? There are times we use an identifying mark, a memory, or perception that sets us apart from another person. There is an image and perception people have about you. We can express individuality in positive ways, and they can be done in unhealthy ways.

Our popular culture screams that you must be distinguishably unique or you must follow someone who is. Products we buy, perfume we wear, music we listen to, styles we dress in, and cars we drive are all ways we try to establish our identifying mark. We try to create an idea and image that will help people to connect with us.

Celebrities and business marketing executives often go to extreme to promote themselves, because there is money to be made if someone identifies with you. High school students often express individuality because they want a sense of control in the social scene. A young mother may grab hold of products or make distinguishable purchases because she may feel like her identity is taking a lower priority to the demands of her family.

There are times we express individuality as a way to mask pain. I've witnessed a woman dye her hair red and wear loud clothing as an outlet to her current pain from the pressure she felt to be perfect as a child. I've seen how a person used expression through plastic surgery as a way to cope with feeling pain from being different. I've met another who wears extremes in fashion as a way to cope with inadequacy.

It is easy to get caught up in a display of individuality in a quest for high self-esteem. How many visitors you get to your personal website, the compliment you hear about your expressive outfit, or the support you feel toward your cause are only a few of the examples of how we do this.

Remember to let go of the high and low of self-esteem. Learn to express individuality in a way that honors self-worth, not self-esteem. Expressing individuality has a pivot point — which you will learn more about in chapter four — meaning you can express yourself positively, or it can be done as a way to cope with misunderstanding self-worth. It can be done out of self-preservation and desperation. It can be done in a way that makes your life better and can help people better know and connect with who you are.

You can learn how to showcase your favorites, connect with style, and develop a personal brand with a sense of self-acceptance.

Self-deception

There are times we sustain our friendships, marriages, and careers by self-deception — believing or living in line with something that is not true. It's hard to know if you're being deceptive when we don't know what is true about ourselves or fail understand sincere traits and emotions.

You can lie to yourself, manipulate others, or use deception to influence the behavior of others. You may rationalize away or justify concepts that are based on your true feelings, real motives, or genuine circumstances.

Self-deception may be convincing yourself you need a new outfit when you don't have any money budgeted for it. Think of ways you justify to make false situations become true. It could be telling yourself your boyfriend loves you when he has told you he wants to break up and he's currently dating other people. It may be saying yes to volunteer at the bake sale when you're already busy, convincing yourself that you need to be there or you won't be a good mom.

To understand this better, start by knowing what deception is: leading a person to believe something that is not true. Self-deception is when you rationalize away something that is real. It is convincing yourself to believe something that is false or misleading.

Authenticity and being real

When I was in sixth grade had a conversation with a very cool ninth grade boy that I wanted to impress. He started talking about how one of his favorite things was music.

"I totally love music," I responded.

"Who's your favorite band?"

I panicked. I didn't know who my favorite band was. The only thing I knew about music was that I used to roller skate in the basement to my mom's Neil Diamond records. I couldn't admit that. So I squirmed my way through the rest of the conversation.

"Oh, I like a lot of things," I turned it on him. "What do you listen to?"

"My favorite bands are U2 and the Cranberries."

I though cranberries were something you ate at Thanksgiving, but I pretended to love cranberries and that other group he was talking about. I let him believe I listened to them all the time. I walked away with the desperate mission: find out about the band *You Two!*

"Be true to yourself." It's a common piece of advice a friend may give. It typically means to not let other people sway you to dishonor your identity (remember identity means heritage, values, traits, choice). It means having the courage to be real.

There are many ways we pretend. In middle school I pretended to like music I had never even heard of. In college I pretended I didn't stay up all night studying when it was time to go to class. When I was dating, I pretended to like baseball much more than I really did.

I have spent five hours cleaning my house, and when company came over I pretended my house never gets dirty. I've pretended I was "fine" when really I felt like going back to bed to cry. I've pretended I was experiencing happiness and success when really I had been experiencing rejection and frustration.

At my first big speech I pretended it was something I did every day, when really I was scared to death. I've pretended to know and eat food varieties. I spotted the word couscous on a dinner menu. With no clue, I pretentiously said, "Oh, look, they have couscous here, how delicious." (It's small grain pasta, like rice.)

Having the courage to be real is difficult. Being real means that we can answer people honestly. We don't have to hide sincere emotions. It doesn't mean that we have to tell every person, every emotion we are feeling when they ask, "How are you?" Sometimes that is just a way of saying hello.

Being real doesn't mean that you use your emotions

to manipulate people or scare them away. Being real doesn't mean you should divulge every personal detail of your life. Have you ever been around someone who said something like, "My dog died, I'm sad, I only have ten dollars in my bank account, I'm feeling bloated today, and I have a doctor's appointment for my foot fungus in an hour." Sometimes too much personal information is scary.

Being authentic means you are honest, not emotional. To be real doesn't mean you divulge socially inappropriate details. Being real is learning how to answer truthfully, without the fear of what other people will think. If I could redo the middle school conversation I had about music, I would admit that I love music, but this time I would simply admit I want to find some new groups to listen to instead of pretending I already knew the hottest bands.

We want to share our best and we want people to like us, to see us as competent. We don't want others to see our worst. It's hard to admit we don't know information. Sometimes we get caught up in perfectionism. We want to be credible so we pretend. Other times we use partial truths.

Sometimes we pretend and act "as if" because we don't know what it feels like to be real. To figure life out sometimes we try expressions and actions to see if they fit. When we're confused about our traits and values, we may come across as fake. There are times it's easier to role-play our way through social situations than it is to explore what it means to be real.

People respect sincerity and honesty. Sometimes it feels scary to be real, but you'll also find that as you share your genuine thoughts, people develop a stronger connection to you, especially as you share your struggles and imperfections.

We disconnect from people we think are perfect. On the outside we may try and impress them but on the inside we detach ourselves from them. They isolate us. They make us feel inadequate. Yet if we hear a personal story of pain, loss, effort, or embarrassment we connect. We pull closer to people who live authentically. We admire them. If they can get through it, we can get through it. We don't feel so alone. They make us feel like we are enough.

Have you ever met someone who allowed you to see in, even revealing their imperfections? It's precious. It's a privilege to know someone who exposes their soul to you. It's a revered moment because we are surrounded by people who are guarded. People are trying to protect themselves. People are trying to put their best self forward in order to have more opportunities. You have been conditioned to think that to be likable and successful you must be perfect. We must be warm, fuzzy, talented, smart, capable, and credible so we hide what is real. Fear controls authenticity. To be authentic, you must be willing to expose your weaknesses. Don't be afraid to share your flaws. Being real is cherished.

Authenticity is the ability to share personal truth, to be honest. Be genuine by acknowledging your thoughts and feelings in your daily actions. Be original by not letting fear of what other people may think lead you choose something that dishonors your heritage, values, traits, or choices.

An Identity Grid example

Put it all together. I know who I am. Write your own simple paragraph.

I am Margie's granddaughter. I believe in kindness and being on time. I am a mother. I am a self-worth researcher. I make great chocolate chips cookies. I have brown hair and brown eyes. I laugh at classic jokes. I thrive on being efficient. I want to be happy. I want to sincerely see other people.

This is just a glimpse of my own Identity Grid. Don't make it complex. Think it through, write it down, and map out your own responses.

Make a list that explains your own Identity Grid: heritage, values, traits, and choices. Take a moment to answer the following questions.

Heritage: Where do you come from?
Values: What do you believe in?
Traits: What do you do?
Traits: What are you like?
Traits: What do you look like?
Choices: What do you want to be?

Understanding Self-Worth

Why did I feel like I had my life put together one minute, then in the next, feel desperate and alone?

Chapter 3

Somebody Please Decode this Emotional Roller Coaster

Have you ever been with a group of women while trying to figure out what food you should eat? Just picture it. The shifty eyes and the question, "What are you going to order?"

I was involved in cheerleading activities through high school and into college. While in college I had an away regional basketball tournament and had been traveling on a bus with nine other girls. We woke up at a hotel and met in the lobby for continental breakfast.

Being all somewhat self-conscious about the calories we should eat in one another's presence, we were generous with the fruit and low-fat yogurt while avoiding the carb-filled bagels. After finishing breakfast we loaded on the bus. We drove three hours to get to our event. We cheered for a four-hour game, doing athletic activity like tumbling, jumping, and stunting.

I missed lunch. Our squad got back on the bus, and we traveled to another hotel. I had a granola bar in my bag and nibbled on that during the long drive. At five o'clock I was feeling faint.

By the time we pulled into a restaurant, it was nine

o'clock at night. I was starving. My stomach sounded like a snarling T. rex. You know, that sound you get when your stomach announces it's empty, where you quickly fold your arms over your guts hoping no one notices the thunder?

I looked at the menu and picked what I wanted to eat. I was ravenous and set out to order the chicken fried streak with mashed potatoes, cream gravy, and a roll. I was even dreaming about pecan pie and chocolate landslide cake. The waitress started taking orders.

"What can I get for you?"

The first girl ordered. "I'll have chicken fingers and fries." Sounds good, right?

The next girl was the captain of the team. The waitress glanced her way, and she ordered.

"I'll *totally* just have salad. Like, I'm so hungry." The orders from my fellow team members continued.

"Salad."

"Salad."

"Salad."

"Salad."

"Salad."

"Salad." I ordered salad.

"Salad."

"Salad."

Now, I'll admit. Salad is very refreshing and there are times you want to eat a cool crisp salad. In this situation I did not want salad. I ordered salad because of the social pressure and because I was worried how my thighs were going to look in the morning.

To understand the emotional roller coaster, put yourself into this story as the one girl who ordered chicken fingers and fries. If everyone else around you ordered a salad and you were the only one who ordered something different, something with a higher calorie count, how would you feel?

That night, the girl that ordered chicken fingers expressed with desperation, "Why didn't you all tell me you were ordering salad? I feel like such a fatty."

She was not the only person feeling low. As I pushed the leafy greens around my plate, I recognized my heart was heavy. The hungry ache in my stomach was nothing compared to the pain in my heart. Why couldn't I choose something different than the rest of the team? As I pictured taking a bite of chicken fried steak smothered in tangy gravy, I wondered why I felt guilt. I felt empty and unsatisfied. Not the kind of dissatisfaction that could be soothed with nutrients, but an emotional frustration that was filled with extremes.

Why did I feel like I had my life put together one minute, then in the next, feel desperate and alone? In that salad moment I felt "fat" and inadequate. How is it that earlier in the day, when I was on the basketball court in my cheerleading uniform, I felt "skinny" and important? How could I feel such extreme emotions in one day?

The core reason we feel extreme emotional highs and lows comes when we base our worth on an exterior changing element. You can group this struggle into eight basic elements that can explain this. The emotional roller coaster is an outcome of misunderstanding self-worth.

From feeling like you've got it together to feeling abandoned, we are constantly being emotionally tested. Hormones and the highs and lows of life are partly to blame for the emotional roller coaster. But there are eight elements that impact how you feel that you have control over. The extreme highs and lows of self-worth can be worked through by understanding the Pivotal Eight.

The Pivotal Eight
1. Appearance
2. Achievements
3. Intelligence
4. Ideals
5. Relationships
6. Recognition
7. Money and Possessions
8. Addiction

We use these eight categories to define our worth. This will help explain almost every high and low self-worth related struggle we have.

Pivot one: Appearance

Being beautiful, appealing, and physically attractive is often an element people associate with worth. Beauty can be defined differently for each culture, each region, and each individual. Yet, we often think there is one perfect, beautiful look that we need to conform to. We need to be skinny, have high end fashion, the latest hair style, or be physically admired by others in order to fit into a category of beautiful. Beauty can include color, shape, proportions, details, and textures that we would designate as appealing, typically referencing our sense of sight.

Elements of appearance include body shape, body size, body type, weight gain, diet, hair style, clothing, fashion sense, proportioned facial features, exercise, flawless skin, the ability to look young when you're older, and staying up-to-date. Beauty perceptions, beauty know-how, being prettier than, or feeling plain are all a part of the appearance category.

Pivot two: Achievements

What do you do? It's a question we answer as part of everyday conversations. It's even a question that is a part of the Identity Grid. Go a little deeper. It is an element we rely on heavily to tell us whether we are important or not. Performance, involvement, achievement, and success seem to weigh heavily on our perceptions of worth. There are times we think the busier we are, the more important we are. We may think if we have a track record of success, then will we be of worth. We've got to prove, demonstrate, show, and leave a paper trail of how incredible we are before we will accept that we have worth. What are our accomplishments?

Elements of achievements may include resumes, to-do lists, awards, performance, abilities, talents, and being able to display success. It can include being associated with an organization, company, team, group, or sport.

Pivot three: Intelligence

Knowledge is very powerful. There are many good things that come from education. There are also many circumstances where we count ourselves out because we don't feel we have the education and intelligence necessary to be a person of worth.

We may not fully participate in classroom settings because of the intimidation of saying the wrong thing, someone might have a better answer, fear of judgment, and overall we may not feel smart enough. There is a common perception that no matter how hard we try, there is always going to be someone else who knows more, who has more experience.

Elements of intelligence may include how smart you feel, your comfort responding intellectually, academic level, degrees, diplomas, experience, certification, and being in a classroom setting.

Pivot four: Ideals

We often feel we need to be excellent in every way possible, otherwise we cannot hold ourselves in high regard. We need to recognize that is okay to have faults, imperfections, and undesirable circumstances. We are still a person of value even if we are not meeting every expectation of being ideal.

This category covers not only the quest to put on the perfect front, but the tender moments of our lives that have not gone well. Even those painful moments of abuse, divorce, bankruptcy, or mental illness can be covered in the category of ideals.

Elements of ideals can include perfect circumstances, from organizing our pantry to letting the neighbors think you have a flawless home life. Think about the ways we try to make everything appear ideal. It may be pretending we are okay when we are not, holding on to the pain from less than ideal circumstances, and letting the concepts of being imperfect, defected, or damaged define who we are.

Pivot five: Relationships

From marriage, family, and dating to friends, coworkers, peers, and neighbors, the relationships we have deeply impact our lives. There are times we use the connection we have with people determine whether we are important or not. How we talk to, behave, and connect with one another can become a major factor to feeling high or low.

Elements of relationships may include having someone to spend time with, seeking love, feeling approval, having someone to talk to, having harmony with the people we love, getting an affirmation of support, having friendships, connecting with someone who cares about you, dealing with conflict, trying to please others, the nature of communication with the people around us, or the emotional connection we have with others. It includes, dating, marriage, and family connections as well as social, community, and peer interactions.

Pivot six: Recognition

It seems like a lot of people are waiting, and hoping,

for their big break. It might be that moment where another person sees us, acknowledges our existence, and publicly points out, "This person matters."

This is not just happening in the entertainment industry, but in our homes, communities, churches, and careers on more simple levels. We let opinion, the positions we hold, and being seen and understood by another person determine whether we have merit or not.

Elements of recognition include status, position, approval, and opinion. It includes perception of opinion, fame, compliments, reputation, or social standing. It is the need to be seen or acknowledged. It might also incorporate what people say about you, fitting in to popular culture, personal judgment, or simply hearing someone say, "Thank you."

Pivot seven: Money and Possessions

From precious knickknacks to big houses, the things you own are common definitions for influence and prestige. The style of your car, the brand of clothing you wear, and the type of income you have can all play a role in how you feel about yourself. Just as money doesn't always lead to happiness, money doesn't always mean high self-esteem.

Elements of money and possession include socioeconomic class, financial power, the size and location of your home, your paycheck, the car you drive, having convenience of life, the cost and brand of your possessions, where you shop, and how you spend your money.

Pivot eight: Addiction

Initially when you hear the word *addiction*, you may think about the habits or dependencies of another person, not yourself. Think about your life. Think about what you rely on daily. What do you devote your time to? What do you look to for emotional support? These daily reliances can be used as a source of comfort in order to feel a degree of personal importance.

Elements of addiction can include shopping, chocolate, cell phones, makeup, alcohol, entertainment, food, pornography, soda, social media, text messaging, compliments, spending money, and technology. It includes any concept that you devote significant time and energy to.

These eight elements help explain the highs and lows. They are at the root of how we are constantly rating ourselves. The Pivotal Eight are the basis for the emotional roller coaster. When we base our worth on any of these eight concepts, we will be strictly limited to their success or failure. When they're up, we're feeling up. When they're low, we're feeling low.

Think about a day you had time to get ready, you were wearing one of your favorite outfits, and you feel beautiful. You feel good. What happens when someone else walks in, and you feel like they look better than you do? You're suddenly discouraged and depressed.

Picture the girl who made the soccer team, and plays varsity. She feels important. Then she gets injured and can't play for a couple of months. She feels down.

Picture this same soccer player recovering and playing all through high school. She gets a college scholarship. After two years as a collegiate athlete, the team cuts her. She is no longer a scholarship soccer player. She feels lost. She feels low.

After being in a high school setting, I have seen the most beautiful, talented, outstanding students come in and try out for a team, a sport, a school play, and a choir group. I've witnessed these students get turned away. I watched them walk away thinking they were worthless.

This doesn't just happen in high schools. I've seen beautiful, talented, outstanding adults use the messages in modern culture to tell them they are useless.

Think about a mom who didn't go to college. What does she think to herself when she sees another woman with a graduate degree? Consider someone who is always trying so hard to come across as perfect.

How do you feel when you have someone to connect with who understands you? Now how do you feel when the most precious relationships in your life have conflict? What if someone notices you? If you live in a small apartment on the wrong side of the tracks and can't even afford a car, does it impact you?

Prove your worth

One moment we may feel like an important and capable person. The next moment we may feel like we are not good enough. We may feel lost, hopeless, and assume we are going to fail. We may try to change things in order to feel good about ourselves.

We create difficult expectations for ourselves in that we should have a distinguishable skill. We should excel at singing, interior design, or gardening. We need to know how to make homemade cleaner, or bake cookies with glow-in-the-dark frosting.

We should be able to create a double-French-twist hair braid, crochet pot holders, be a world class photographer, run a successful home-based business, be the master chef of a new Artichoke Swiss Chicken recipe, or know how to juggle marshmallows while riding a unicycle. There is pressure to host themed garden parties, with matching table cloths and delicate party favors. We may feel like we need to be a published author, design the latest hair bow for girls, keep a trend setting scrapbook, or have a magazine cover laundry room. We allow ourselves to feel bad about all the things we cannot do.

We may feel like the more things we have on our to-do list the more important we are. If we can balance a day with a part-time job, attend a PTA meeting, cheer on a child on at a baseball game, and prepare homemade dinner without so much as getting flustered, then we are important. Most of the time we end up over-scheduled and overwhelmed.

Most of the time, we are measuring our talents up against the talents of others. We watch, mimic, and social-media-follow the abilities of others and mentally tear ourselves down if our skills are not putting us in the "important" category. There are lifetime achievement awards, employee-of-the-month plaques, and mother-of-the-year expectations. Gold statues, gold stars, and gold medals get distributed to the best. But we are often failing to celebrate extraordinary unseen efforts. When it comes to titles, visual display of talents, and awards, we can put a lot of pressure on ourselves.

A person's level of value is not founded on talents. It is false to associate busy with self-worth. Success does not automatically mean self-esteem. It is wrong to look only at documented intelligence to determine our importance. You don't need to be a designated woman-of-the-year, a television personality, a search-engine-optimized blogger, or have a compelling two-page resume to be important. The more achievements you have does not equate to how important you are.

Your worth does not come from the makeup you wear, what people say about you, how successful your marriage is, whether or not you've been on a cruise, and if you've been seen, selected, or complimented.

Identify the highs and lows

You have the biggest most luxurious home on the block and a high-paying job. Then you quit your job in order to be a mother and a new neighbor builds a bigger house next to yours. Your sense of value drops.

You buy a designer pair of jeans and get a new blouse in the color of the year. But spring rolls in a new set of colors. Suddenly you are out of date and feel frumpy.

You get married at age twenty-eight. You are happy and feel young and in love. At age thirty-seven, the dynamic of your marriage changes. Your relationship did not turn out how you expected it would. You are feeling older, average, and insignificant.

You rely on technology on a daily basis to feel connected and liked. No one is responding to you, and you feel empty.

Extreme emotions can happen in appearance, achievements, intelligence, ideals, relationships, recognition, possessions, and addictions. When we base our worth on exterior, changing things, no matter how hard we try, our efforts will never be enough. The first thing we need to do is recognize how and when we are rating ourselves. If we are not aware that we are basing our worth on exterior, changing things, then we are at the mercy of the Pivotal Eight elements.

Stop keeping score

When you are keeping score and rating yourselves, it implies our value is changing or that there is a winner and a loser. If you can recognize that your worth as a person is already established, you won't need to look to fashion, opinion, possessions, or awards to determine where you stand. You can be at peace about your identity and recognize what is happening. Your worth is not based on appearance, achievements, opinion, ideals, intelligence, possessions, or addictions.

When we keep score by measuring ourselves to another, it either puts us above or below another person. It offers no long-term peace. It can make us vain or it can make us bitter. Any validation we get from a comparison will only last a short while. Keeping score, social competition, and comparison is rooted in insecurity.

Remember the labels of high self-esteem and low self-esteem. We are conditioned to keep score, to rate ourselves as a good person or a bad person. Stop. The consequence of constantly ranking yourself against another person is inadequacy. As long as you're keeping score, you will find you're never going to be good enough. Self-improvement and goal setting is one thing, keeping score and establishing a hierarchy is quite another. Be the best that you can be, and if you have a bad day, try again tomorrow.

Our worth does not come from having status, being better than another, being in a higher position, or in taking a count of success. Self-worth is constant. If you live in a way that honors this, you can stop fighting for recognition and start giving it to others.

How to level out the emotional roller coaster

There are three concepts you can use to level out the emotional roller coaster. I know who I am. I accept myself. I sincerely see and celebrate others.

Trust in your identity. Know who you are. Pay attention to the Identity Grid. Know how to answer the questions that explain your identity. Because it is always changing, it is important to understand what makes you up. This helps prevent confusion. The more you understand yourself, the better prepared you will be for success.

Agree and find harmony with your identity. I accept myself. There is more information to come on self-acceptance in chapter six, but there is a continual process we need to recognize our weaknesses without resenting them.

Consciously avoid rating yourself and other people. It will take constant attention. Start noticing the lives of other people, not as a competitive gauge, but as a way to learn their struggles and build empathy.

The extremes

There is a battle of extremes — two directions we can go when we do not understand self-worth. Some people will make a bold, loud, aggressive stance when they feel insignificant. Other people resort to staying quiet. They may have passive responses, indecision, and sometimes they just give in.

On one side we can lean toward vanity. We may wear eccentric clothing, tout conceit, make claims how much better we are, and can become entitled and walk around with the attitude that we deserve every good thing. We may try to make statements about how awesome we are and how unimportant others are not. On this end the core principle is excessive concern, seeking for an advantage, and display of self.

Then there is self-defeat. Eyes are lowered and hearts tend to give up. There are times we almost give up, resign ourselves to never being someone who matters, let insignificance win, and accept the idea of being secondary. We may accept the idea that we're worthless, average, and meaningless.

Picture a girl at a residential treatment center with half-shaved haircut dyed jet black with a red highlight.

In a class of thirty she's constantly speaking up, making loud, witty comments, struggling for power. She's publicly shouting her opinions as if her life depended on it.

She later confided, "I don't want to feel invisible. I spent years being invisible and forgotten during my parents' divorce. I feel like I need to show people that I'm here, and I've got something to share." She was taking a bold stance to tell people she matters.

It's time to start thinking and acting more positively about self-worth. We don't need to keep score. Evaluations, judgments, and critics cause us to stay on guard and treat life like a competition. We need to be aware of how we are feeling, and we need to recognize the thoughts and situations that make us feel badly. But we don't need to keep score, outdo, and compete to establish that we are a person of worth. We need to let go of all the proving and recognize our worth is already established.

It is time to let go of your score sheet, the ranking, competing, and thinking we are at war. It is time to pivot.

Understanding Self-Worth

You must learn how to pivot.
Learn how to see the good in each
of these eight categories and stop
living in emotional desperation.

Chapter 4

Pivot Point

My body dissatisfaction started in high school and surged when I got to college. My body, my face, and my hair never seemed to look good enough. I took inventory of all the food in my apartment so I would know the exact calorie count. I remember running on a treadmill with tears streaming down my face. I was spending almost four hours a day in the gym. My body was in prime condition, yet I hated it. I loathed my body. My body always seemed to be a disappointment.

I know I'm not alone in having felt discouraged about my body. One of the most common complaints from women is "I am not happy when I look in the mirror."

One night, while studying with some classmates at the local pizzeria, I was feeling upset. Tired and overwhelmed, I felt like I would never be skinny enough. I had another slice of pizza thinking, "Why does it even matter what I eat?" I ate another, then another. I was being soothed by eating. As soon as the bite was gone, I felt empty again. I ended up emotionally eating five pieces of pizza, while my peers were chatting, seeming to enjoy the food. They had no idea I was struggling.

When I got back to my apartment, I went into the bathroom, crumpled on the floor, and cried. With a tear stained face I looked at the toilet.

"I could stick my finger down my throat." My thoughts were blaring.

I wondered if it could clear away my guilt and disappointments. I looked into the toilet bowl. Then I thought about my parents. It was enough to make me stop. I knew making myself throw up wasn't right. But I also knew the pain I was feeling in the core of my soul also wasn't right.

I washed my face and left the bathroom. I wanted to know why I was hurting. I was upset. In that moment I developed a determination to make sense of it. In the coming days I found myself having conversations with some very dear friends, and I made a powerful discovery. I was not alone. I was not the only person who felt bad about how I looked. I started reading. From the college library to professional articles to bible verses, I was hungry to soak in anything I could about body image.

I felt something that has forever changed my struggle with body image. It wasn't instant or perfect, but I kept getting a glimpse of a message. My body is the very essence of my life. I cannot experience a full sense of joy without my body. To have a body is to live. A body — my body — is good. The ability to see, smell, hear, taste, touch, and sense is miraculous.

This was a pivot point. Something as small as a new way of thinking changed how I lived. Over the next six months I was unknowingly putting in effort to see my body as something to care for, to enjoy. I developed a pattern. One tiny moment at a time I started to stop desperately seeking my worth through my body and allowed my body to be good. My appearance became something revered and respected.

Instead of seeing my body as something that must be skinny, beautiful, and perfect, I simply thought of my body as important. My hands lift, my toes point, my eyes see, my abdomen is the home to my vital organs. My lips smile, my mouth tastes, and my ears hear. A time in life where I once felt so uncomfortable became a time of life where I felt profound joy.

I would put on my backpack and make the ten-minute uphill walk from my apartment to campus. I could feel the weight of the books on my shoulders with gratitude. I would look at the trees, feel the air expand my lungs, and pay attention to the slight burn in my chest from walking. It felt good.

Standing under the lights of a sold-out regional basketball tournament I remember feeling the pulse of the crowd chanting as if in rhythm with my heartbeat. Beads of sweat formed as if part of the air. Standing on the sidelines, I bent my knees, jumped back, and felt the bounce of the gym floor on my palms as I completed a back handspring. I looked up at the crowd and felt profound joy at what my body could experience.

Pouring a bowl of cereal in the morning was a good experience. I watched the milk slosh. I tasted every sweet bite. I felt my stomach being soothed, and my body being energized. I stopped counting calories and weighing myself. Instead of seeing my thighs as big I noticed how they were strong. They helped me walk. My stomach wasn't fat. It was important. My skin wasn't flawed. It was a miraculous.

If you know how important, how precious, how delicate, and how powerful your body is you care for it. You dress it, you exercise it and you fuel it like to matters, because it does.

This altered thinking has become sharper over time. I seek this pivot point out. I now purposely live in a way where appearance becomes something good. My body is strong, marvelous, and valued. This understanding changes everything for me. Because my body is good, I care for it. I see it as precious. This means that health and fashion have an important role to play in my life. They care for this precious body.

I have learned through personal experience what it takes to overcome the extreme highs and lows from body dissatisfaction. You can experience it too. Do you know what it means to have a body?

Have you ever felt the bliss of singing off-key in the car, doing cartwheels in the grass, or simply walking up the stairs? There is so much joy to be found in your body. Consider what it means to hug a friend, skip with a child, take a deep breath, sit on the floor, or kiss someone you love. Go ahead, fill your lungs with air. Blink. Snap. Roll your shoulders. Wiggle your toes. Touch your hands and pay attention to the softness of your skin. The ability to feel is precious. Isn't it cool?

I met a woman who was bound to a wheelchair and still found complete joy in living. She had been through a car accident that left her paralyzed from the waist down. Here was someone who had lost some of the use of part of her body, yet she was happy. She looked me in the eyes and expressed the sheer joy it was to have a body. She pointed out all the things her body could do. Her body gives her life.

A pivot point is the moment (no matter whether you're aware of it or not) where you let any element become the source of your worth and the only reason you're important, or it becomes a supplement to life. You allow this element to make your life good or bad.

Explore the Pivotal Eight so you can better see how this works. Appearance, achievements, intelligence, ideals, relationships, recognition, money, and addiction all have the ability to be a source for good or they can become the driving definition of worth. They can be something to look forward to, or they can be the cause of heartache and extreme emotions. You must learn how to pivot. Learn how to see the good in each of these eight categories and stop living in emotional desperation. Establish pure motives.

The Appearance Pivot:
Go back to the early 1990s. My favorite outfit was a set of bright pink units. It was a cotton-poly-knit, one-piece shift dress, complete with a stretchy set of mix-and-match belts and spandex pants. I had a claw for bangs. I would pull my bangs flat, spray them with hairspray and use the curling iron to sizzle them into a back curl. It was offset by batwings that consisted of backcombing the sides of my hair to look like it could fly.

I once met a woman who claimed to have the biggest hair on the planet. I believe her. She used two sets of hot rollers on her hair. It was so big it didn't even fit in her yearbook picture. She was on top of her game.

What would happen today if the woman with the biggest-hair-on-the-planet walked into your local high school with a frantic desire of fitting in? How would she feel? What would happen if today I walked into a circle of competitive moms wearing my pink units and batwings with a frantic desire of feeling accepted? It will all depend on your motives, your confidence, and how much you are basing your worth on appearance. Most of the time, out-of-date trends make us feel like we are not good enough. It goes back to the roller coaster concept of emotional highs and lows.

Appearance can be good, exciting, healing, and it can support self-worth. Now, pivot. Appearance can be desperate, unhealthy, slave-like, and can constantly demand effort you don't have.

What do you do to keep up your appearance? Some people take a monthly visit to the salon, buy new clothes, or stop at the makeup counter for a limited-time-only fall color. Daily, you may shower, put on moisturizer, blow dry your hair, get dressed, or brush your teeth. At what level are you supposed to care for yourself?

Each person will have an individual response based on their lifestyle, but start paying attention to how you can have a positive relationship with appearance. Make decisions that are in line with a healthy pivot. Let appearance become something that makes your life good, not something you must desperately have in order to be important. My favorite definition of a beautiful woman came from my mom who said, "I think a beautiful woman is someone who takes care of herself." How do you take care of yourself?

Explore your motives. Think about your personal reason why. Why do you take a shower in the morning? We brush our teeth to have a clean mouth and so we don't get cavities. Extend your motives beyond a shower or teeth brushing. Think about you're the last piece of clothing you bought for yourself. Why did you buy it?

I recently bought a gray jacket. I got it because I've been looking for a new one to replace a worn-out jacket. I needed something warm, it was on sale, it was soft, and I felt like it fit my personality. All okay motives. Now I'll admit, I once bought an on-trend blouse in the talked-about style of the year, the peplum. It was a shirt with an extra ruffle around the waist. The experts said, "It will make you look thinner and draw attention to your little waist."

I stopped to think about why I bought that shirt. It wasn't because I liked it or needed it. I bought the shirt so I would be noticed. It was so I could be seen as someone on trend. This was an unhealthy pivot because I was using the shirt to define my value. I don't even like the peplum style. The experts say I will feel slender and feminine, but I felt like the extra ruffle made me feel poufy and awkward. I hated it, but I bought it anyway. Look at the ways we frantically base our worth on our appearance.

"I am only important if my clothing is high end and always on trend."

"I have to get my hair done. No one can see me if my hair is not done. I can't go into public without makeup on."

"I have to have a slim waistline."

"Right after I have a baby, I must fit back into my pre-baby clothes."

"I exercise to be skinny."

It encourages emotions of panic, anxiety, crash dieting, plastic surgery, credit card debt, makeup counter dependence, disappointment, and struggles with food. Pivot instead by looking at ways appearance is positive, good, and fun.

"I take care of myself."

"Getting my hair cut was fun, and it inspired me."

"I put on makeup in the morning as part of my self-care routine. It accentuates my good features."

"I exercise to be healthy."

"I bought a dress that fits my personality. I can express who I am, and I love it. It makes me excited to wear it, and I feel comfortable."

Do you have a healthy relationship with fashion?

The way you dress is important. It's an expression of how you want other people to see you and treat you. Fashion can be used as a form of self-care, to send a message, to build credibility, to express style, and it can be plain fun. How you dress will impact how you feel about yourself. Fashion can be good, very good.

Roman emperors, Egyptian kings, and royalty in medieval Europe are all known for making purple a hot trend based on uncommon resources and social class. Purples and blues were rare pigments that the lower class could not afford and often had the same value as gold. People once had to go to great lengths to acquire the color dye through rare natural minerals or mollusks. Brown, gray, and tan came from surface soils and earth tones. Those colors were more available and therefore associated with the lower class. If you wore purple, it demonstrated your status. It established your importance.

Fashion can create a hierarchy. It can create pain. Styles can be used to put people on a level, make money, and establish authority. It is an industry. Where there is someone with an inside edge for staying up-to-date, there is usually someone who is left out. Trend, by nature, is exclusive. Not everyone can or will participate. We can fall prey to the glitz and glam. Not always because it is inspiring or pretty, but because we are told it is what will make us more important and desirable as a person. Think about the money and time you are putting into fashion. It's unhealthy if you are putting clothing and accessories before relationships.

Businesses rely on new ideas and fresh design in order to turn a profit. Is it bad? No! Consider where trend comes from. It starts with an idea and is usually based on creativity. We can find strength, inspiration, and motivation through creativity. Businesses can't always sell the same things; they evolve and not always for the sake of profit. Sometimes it is to beat boredom, to give people opportunities—a powerful idea, perhaps the most powerful because someone is passionately inspired. Trend can be good for the economy. The mistake comes when we let businesses persuade us that our worth is based on participating in trend. Take the time to recognize marketing and sales strategies before you mindlessly follow fashion.

Society will glamorize and romanticize some of the styles, sizes, and shapes that are the most difficult to obtain. In the early 1800s round curvy figures and pale white skin were in. It meant you could afford to eat and stay indoors. Consider what we want to look like today. Not everyone can make time for or afford to spend hours at the gym a day at the beach, bronzing in the sun.

Clothing styles are always changing. When a new look is released, consider the money, power, and esteem involved. Think about all the designers, buyers, stylist, models, bloggers, critics, and direct sellers that depend on trend. One season we rave about greens, and the next season it is purples. It's the nature of fashion to always look to the next cut, color, and pattern. Being on trend can come at the expense of a person's sense of worth when they don't recognize the business of it. We must learn to see fashion as an industry and not as a requirement for worth.

Fashion also has a pivot point. The clothing you wear can become the source of your worth and a reason why you have value, or you can let it become a positive, good, inspiring aspect of your life. It can be an aspect that supplements your unconditional worth. It is a very fine line. Without realizing it, you may initially choose a pair of shoes and style your hair a certain way with positive motives. Without thinking about it, you can also become a slave to fashion, using style, or even the lack of style, desperately.

Remember to pivot. I've felt sheer excitement over the beauty of a simple black pencil skirt. It almost gives me chills to pair it with the right top. I feel confident when I wear clothing that I love. To slide into a soft jersey T-shirt and a comfy pair of jeans that mold to my body is heaven. I have a favorite dress. My favorite necklace looks like bronze lace. It makes me happy. I love shoes. I have a great go-to structured jacket that I can throw on and go from feeling frumpy to feeling pulled together. Don't forget how good fashion can be.

Is fashion a positive or negative influence in your life? Remember you have unconditional value. Make decisions that will help you have a positive relationship with fashion. Learn how to pivot in each of the eight categories.

The Achievement Pivot:

Prove it. We often try to let people know we matter through how accomplished we are. Sometimes we act like the busier we are, the more important we will be. If we don't have a powerful resume, we think we don't have value.

I have seen some of the most beautiful, talented, outstanding teens try out for a high school team, choir, or school play, and if a coach, judge, or teacher did not put them with the group, they walked away feeling worthless. Our desire to perform well and be accomplished goes beyond high school.

"I am a soccer player. I have to be all-state or I won't really matter."

"I have to write a book in order to be someone."

"Busy, busy busy . . . I have to do it all."

Feelings of worth don't go very far if we don't also develop a sense of purpose. Purpose and goal setting are vital and powerful. Pivot so you achieve a sense of purpose, not to prove that you are good enough.

"I play soccer because it helps me set goals. It gives me something to look forward to. It makes my life good."

"I'm passionate about writing. It has always been a goal of mine to write a book."

"Hard work makes me feel happy and fulfilled."

The Intelligence Pivot:

"We are now teaching three-years-olds to read," exclaimed the radio ad. "Enroll your child in advanced preschool today!" The pressure to be smart starts at birth. Have you ever heard a proud parent say something like, "Baby Ella is already rolling from her back to her stomach, and she can say 'da da.' My child is so smart."

It happens so young. At age five my oldest son was tested and rated going into school. I was sent home a note that showed what percentile he was in compared to every other kindergartener in the district for his letter recognition and rhyming abilities. The elementary school also has a "gifted and talented" program. It is a fantastic program. Even though it helps smart kids get an academic edge there are also children who are getting the message that they are not "gifted and talented." The messages we are surrounded with that tell us we need to be smart to be important.

The Under Pressure Project was one of the most eye-opening studies I have ever done. Over 500 teens were asked to share their biggest pressures. I thought it was going to be predictable. Certainly fitting in was going to be the top pressure. I guessed their stress was going to be related to dating, drugs, body image, or popularity. But it wasn't. By a wide margin the top struggle high school students addressed over and over was the pressure to be smart, to get into college, and to make something of their future. Students were insanely concerned over their academic ability.

In junior high schools, teachers start intimidating students to get straight A's. "Once you hit ninth grade, this is going on your transcript. Your grades are a permanent record. You'll never get into college if you don't do well in school." College applications, standardized testing, and the title of valedictorian are looming. Parents are standing on the sidelines demanding academic excellence. One teen confided, "The stress is so intense I don't know how to relax anymore. I can't afford to slip up in school. My mom is always there, looking over my shoulder, guilting me. She wants me to do my best but I will feel like a complete failure if I don't get a full ride college scholarship."

It doesn't just happen in school systems. I met a woman who was working a great job for a great company. She cried, "I never feel smart enough. I always feel like someone out there is smarter than me."

What do you know? Do you remember people's names? Do you raise your hand confidently in a class? Are you seen by others as an expert? Your expertise may be in plants, child care, theater, music, woodworking, nature, or psychology. You may study how to cook, craft, and create. Proficiency can be developed with numbers, words, science, or art. You may know how to make people laugh, how to be a good friend, or the latest information in popular culture.

Do you know that the sun rises in the east and sets in the west? At what degree does water freeze? How many players are on a football team? How many keys does a piano have? What is a cumulus cloud? What color is trending in fall fashion? How do you publish a website? What is an acute triangle? How do you apply eye shadow to create a smoky eye? What were the reviews for the movie that came out this weekend? Can you quote from the Bible? What year was George Washington born? It sometimes seems like the more we know, the more important we are.

"I'm only important if I can get a college scholarship."

"I must have the correct answer when I raise my hand in class."

"Someone else is smarter than me."

"I don't have my college degree like they do."

Intelligence has a pivot. Stop using knowledge

as something to beat yourself down with. Start seeing the good. Knowledge is one of the most powerful components in the world. Information can inspire you. Learning is thrilling and healing. Intelligence can fill your life with so much joy. Knowledge will help you understand self-worth.

"I love learning about history. It is inspiring to find out what happened years ago."

"Reading is one of my favorite things to do."

"I love learning what the Anderson family does to teach their children. It gives me ideas and helps me be a better parent."

Sometimes we don't participate fully in knowledge because we may feel like someone else has a better answer, we may feel more comfortable on the sidelines, or we may worry about what others will think. Simply remember that your comments and experiences are needed. Remember how good knowledge is. Remember people need to learn from you.

You have experiences no one else has had. There are words that only you can share. Do you know how much you are needed? No matter whether it is the walls of your own home or somewhere in the community, your knowledge is deeply needed. Never let yourself feel like you are not smart enough.

The Ideals Pivot:

It was the perfect summer day for a family picnic at the lake. I was in charge of the sandwiches, and I took this responsibility seriously. I went grocery shopping for all the ingredients and planned for delicate croissants, lettuce, quality cheeses, tomatoes, and perfectly sliced meat from the deli counter. As I packed the cooler, I was sure to put in both Miracle Whip and mayonnaise.

As the family gathered around to eat, my sister started to prepare a plate for her kids. I saw her rummage around in the cooler.

"Do you have any cheese?"

I felt the blood drain from my face. I felt panic set in. I forgot the cheese. I left it at home. What was my sister-in law going to think, that we were a family that doesn't eat cheese on their sandwiches? What about the nutritional and flavor value of lunch? What a disaster. No cheese. After all I had planned and envisioned, this picnic was ruined.

I spent the next hour distraught. I thought the entire picnic was ruined until my brother, very brusquely, said, "Karen! It's just cheese. Let it go."

Why was it so difficult to let go of the forgotten cheese? Because I wanted the picnic to be perfect, I had a vision for how this family lunch should turn out. It did not meet my expectations. Instead of adapting to the forgotten cheese, I stewed about it. I mentally tore myself down over it. I allowed myself to think and feel that the entire day was ruined.

We often work very hard to have the perfect life.

"I forgot the cheese."

"I should be married with 2.5 kids, a dog, and own a home with a white picket fence."

"Life didn't turn out how I expected. I'm such a

loser."

"I didn't have a good childhood. How can I be a person of worth when something so horrible happened to me?"

Now pivot in the category of ideals. Instead of stewing over unfulfilled expectations, live for the life you want. Picture it. Work for it. Live for it. But don't berate yourself when something different happens. Let the ideals in your life be something to encourage you, not to be something that excludes you from having value and peace.

"I want to get married and have a family."

"I want my dream job."

"I want a home where people can come and feel safe."

The Relationships Pivot:

I have a very dear friend whose parents went through a divorce while she was in high school. This was a time in her life where her relationships felt shattered. She felt like she mattered less because her parents didn't love each other.

There are so many stages to our life and relationships. Single, married, divorced, unable to have kids, young mother, busy father, single mother, home-alone-while-the-husband-is-constantly-away, empty nester, widowed. Does your relationship status impact your feelings of worth?

After giving a series of presentations to teen girls, I noticed a pattern. I asked them to rate on a scale of one to one hundred how they would feel about themselves in a scenario from the Pivotal Eight. They were asked how they would feel if their clothes were out of date, if they didn't make the team, if they got a low test score. Then, I asked another question.

"How would you feel if the hottest boy at school asked you out on a date? You keep dating. You find out from your best friend he said you are beautiful. How would you feel about yourself?"

The girls reacted by shouting, "One hundred." Some even screamed, "One hundred ten."

"How would you feel if six months later he's not talking to you and he likes your best friend?"

The room hushed. They gasped, "Zero."

A teenage girl's relationships tend to have the most extreme emotional reaction out of any category. This also goes for women and mothers. Having someone to connect with and love can send them to the highest of highs and the lowest of lows. Relationships are the most emotionally explosive worth defining category. There is a gender difference. Both men and women need connections in their lives but women tend to hang onto them like a worth-defining lifeline.

Pay attention to your relationships. This is the most under-talked-about category, and yet it brings the most emotional extremes. This isn't just about family and dating relationships. Friendships powerfully impact our sense of self-worth. Having a person to connect with is a basic human need. The idea of having a friend can influence you in many ways. Watch how any relationship impacts your worth.

"No one wants to hang out with me tonight. I must be a loser"

"I'm only important if I go on a date with him."

"My kids are not making good choices, so I must be a bad mom."

"I don't have anyone to talk to."

This category is difficult because it includes the choices and actions of another. You can't always make that positive pivot alone. We must work through our struggles with the person we are connected with. Don't let the decisions of another person lead you to think you don't have value. Work at your relationships. They take effort, constant effort. Find ways to let them be good.

"I will always cherish the relationship with my mom."

"Marriage is precious."

"I love laughing with my sisters."

The Recognition Pivot:

We like to be acknowledged, to have approval, and to be widely accepted. Fame and reputation seem to be a widely sought after trait because we internalize it to mean we're desirable. If people want to be around us, if they like our talents, if they see us, only then can we accept that we're valuable.

Popularity can be explained. I met a preteen girl at a back-to-school workshop who was frantically looking for some secret to make all her popularity dreams come true. She asked, "Can you tell me how to be popular?"

There is no mystical solution, but there are skills. One thing all popular people have in common is a belief in their ability to influence their peers, for good or bad. Popular people may also have an awareness of current culture and trends. Popular people may also have something others want or be in a position of recognition.

But to be popular in high school, in your neighborhood, in your career, or anywhere else, you don't need to frantically scramble, constantly research the latest movement, or alter your personality. Instead of focusing on the word *popular*, why don't you consider the word *leader*?

To be a leader you must simply believe in your ability to influence your peers. Yes, some people will have a more quiet personality, but they can still believe in their ability to influence others. Look at these recognition examples.

"I've got to be popular."

"Nobody said anything about my outfit today, so I must be a loser."

"I spent all day cleaning, cooking, and organizing, and no one even cares."

"I'm talented. Why can't anyone see it? I feel invisible."

"I have to hear affirmations from others; I rely on them."

When we are free from the opinions of others — the good opinions and the bad opinions — then we are free to be ourselves. Recognition doesn't have to be desperate. Pivot.

"I am going to stand up for what I believe in."

"I'm going to compliment other people."

"I want to influence others for good."

The Money and Possessions Pivot:

Stuff, it's everywhere. There is crafted home décor, knickknacks, and the little plaque that says "Home Sweet Home." Think about all the toys, games, dolls, building sets, and the puzzles spread across our homes. There are kitchen mixers, the expensive brand of paper towels, television sets, sound systems, mp3 players, smart phones, and all the latest gadgets. We look at cars, boats, motor homes, campers, trailers, snowmobiles, and jet skies. There are shoes, jeans, blouses, dresses, suits, and purses with name brand labels.

It's not just about the all the possessions we own. There is also a direct relation between the amount of money you have and the amount of value and importance you feel.

"I don't have a paycheck; I'm only a stay-at-home mom. I have nothing tangible that tells me I have value."

"I can only wear designer labels."

"My sister keeps telling me to go on a cruise. She can't believe we've never had that experience. We can't afford it. We'll never be that couple that gets to go on nice vacations."

"I was laid off from my job. I feel worthless because I can't pay the bills."

Even our possessions have a pivot. They can be desperately needed and become something we base our value on. They can also be something that makes life better.

"I'm so thankful for my KitchenAid mixer. I can bake faster."

"We have a boat. It brings the people we love together to do something we enjoy."

"I love putting a wreath on my front door. I love making this house my own."

"Earning money, working hard, and saving money is rewarding."

"I like to wear clothes that are good quality. It's so nice to find something that fits me well."

The Addictions Pivot:

Think about what life was like one hundred years ago. I listened to a woman talk about her grandmother's childhood. "It was really hard for her growing up. Not hard like we think about today, but physically it took extreme effort. They had to work for everything. Sometimes we don't realize how many conveniences we have." She then shared how they farmed their own food, carried in their own water, and made their own clothing. Communication was different, shopping was different, entertainment was different, and even the food they ate was different than the lifestyle we live today.

It seems like the fewer physical struggles we have, the more emotional struggles we're opened up to. There is something about hard work that protects us from emotional dependencies. There is something about the conveniences and pleasures of life that we cling to in unhealthy ways. Convenience and the pleasures of life impact feelings of depression.

What do you rely on daily?

Some people mindlessly shop. They spend money they don't have to fill an emotional void. Retail therapy is a term we use to describe shopping with the purpose of feeling better or soothing our emotions. When we use shopping as an outlet to cope, we set ourselves up for continued emotional highs and lows.

After a difficult breakup with her boyfriend, a teen went shopping with her mom. The mom thought a girl's day out complete with a makeover would soothe her daughter's broken heart. It was done out of love. After getting new makeup and expensive clothes the mom said, "We'll show him." As time went on the daughter continued to think she needed new clothes to cope. Any time she felt hurt she went to the mall in search of the right trends to prove she was "somebody." The mother thought she was helping her daughter through a break-up, but she was really setting her daughter up for an unhealthy relationship with shopping. We can buy new things to take care of ourselves, not to establish that we are valuable.

People have extreme relationships with food. Some people self-soothe with chocolate. Some people binge and purge. There are people who rely on exercise, makeup, and fashion. There are people who rely on drugs, pornography, or alcohol.

Entertainment, cell phones, computers, technology, and social media can all become something we look to in order to feel like we have value.

Look at the things you do on a daily basis and decide if you have a healthy relationship with them. What do you need to change?

"I have to check my social media pages. No one liked my comment. I have to get more online friends."

"No one is texting me today."

"I'm depressed. I need some chocolate."

"I hate my life. I need a drink."

"I spend most of my day gaming online. My avatar talks to more people than I do."

Pivot. Let the pleasures and conveniences be elements that make life good. Don't mindlessly go to them in order to feel better about yourself.

"I love my cell phone. I love how I can instantly contact with the people that I care about."

"Let's go catch a movie tonight."

"Technology is amazing."

"There is nothing like eating a well-prepared steak cooked to perfection."

"I bought this scarf as a memento. Anytime I wear it I'm reminded of a great day I had with a great friend.

We are continually making a decision on how we allow appearance, achievements, intelligence, ideals, relationships, recognition, money, and addictions either become the source of our worth or a supplement to our life.

As you recognize you don't need these eight exterior elements to be a person of worth, you can begin to make changes. Instead of basing your worth on appearance, you can find joy in being healthy and taking care of yourself physically. Instead of letting a trophy or to-do list determine whether you are an important person, you can participate in activities that add meaning to your life. When you can let go of the scramble to be smart, fit in, or always have your cell phone, you can find peace and assurance and allow knowledge, friendships, or technology to bring an added contentment to your life.

Confidence is not about being self-centered. It's about being emotionally centered, so you can better see other people.

Chapter 5

What about Me?

Hearing the news made me feel hurt, not happy. I watched a friend get a big visual career opportunity. It was a moment when I should have been happy for her success. I should have called her and congratulated her. I desperately wanted to celebrate her, but I couldn't. Instead of support her during a time she could have used a friend, I turned away from her. Her accomplishment upset me.

I once sat with crossed arms through a class. As I watched the presenter, I felt like her knowledge minimized my own. I didn't even give her a chance because I felt like she threatened my value.

On another occasion I was looking at photographs. The picture looked heavenly. She was sitting in the sunshine on a cruise ship sipping on raspberry lemonade while I was home, in the cold, saving money for my child's dental work. I remember thinking, "I'll never get the chance to go on an exotic vacation. Her life is so much better than mine."

One of my first memories of feeling envy happened in sixth grade when I watched the student council elections. I watched eight of my peers get voted in as leaders. In my mind, they were chosen and accepted while I was not. They had made it, and I had not. They now had an advantage, and I did not. I still had something to prove. It felt like success and self-worth were limited, and if they got it, there wouldn't be enough for me.

Emotions of envy and inadequacy tend to hit me most when I see another person getting an opportunity or having a moment of success. I personalize it. I make it about me when it should be about them. I have let the success of others impact my own feelings of worth. It somehow feels like their success amplifies my failure. It's easy to mistake their opportunity to mean I'm not good enough.

Early on in my self-worth outreach work I got a phone call from a women's conference event planner. She asked if I would participate as a keynote presenter for an upcoming convention. My stomach fluttered at the opportunity. Although I was nervous, I was also excited at the prospect of meeting and interacting with a large group of women. I started preparing months in advance. I thought about the mothers and professionals who would be there and wondered what I could share with them.

One week before the event I got a phone call from the event planner. "Karen, I am sorry but we will need to cancel your presentation."

My mouth dropped as I reached for the calendar.

"Is everything okay?" I asked.

"Oh, it is more than okay," the event planner responded. "We just received word that *Young-American-Super-Business-Woman-to-Watch-Mother-of-the-*

Year (or that is how I heard the event planner say it) just got back from an international tour and she just so happens to have an opening in her schedule to speak at our conference. Her free hour is during your session."

I didn't even have a passport.

The phone call ended with the event planner gushing about the resume of this woman along with her excitement that the conference was now featuring an international superstar. It was as if the event planner thought telling me how great this woman-of-the-year was would compensate for canceling on me.

For an instant I had the thought that my experience, efforts, and my value as a person were threatened by her. She actually had a trophy. She toured the world. She hung out with the important people, and she took my spot. An opportunity that really mattered to me was given to someone who had this kind of experience every day.

I wondered if she would forever be my rival — that person I was just stuck following behind. I hung up the phone feeling like I just wasn't good enough. Did her in-demand lifestyle and title make her better than me?

I had a decision to make, would I let the *Young-American-Super-Business-Woman-to-Watch-Mother-of-the-Year-Who-Just-Got–Back-From-an-International-Tour* be a threat or could I sincerely celebrate her?

After taking a couple of deep breaths, I remembered the concept that self-worth is constant. It is always there and does not change. As I recognized that she does not minimize me, I desperately wanted to stop feeling inadequate. I made a decision to see and celebrate her — a decision I knew would not be instant or easy. It was a decision that would take continual reminders that she did not dissolve me. Her success did not minimize me. Her worth did not take away from my own.

Anytime you have a problem with another person's success, you're really having a problem understanding your own self-worth.

The role of other people and your self-worth

It is your challenge to live without feeling like others are constantly threatening your self-worth. You engage in an unspoken battle with every interaction you have. We mindlessly gauge, "How do I measure up, fit in with, and relate to you?"

Your boss at work may have a higher standing, your neighbor may have less money, your sister is prettier, your friend has a better resume, and you may have the nicer home. It's not really talked about, but we internalize a class system. We instinctively and unconsciously take everyone else's lives very personally.

There is no security in trying to understand our self-worth through the lives of other people. It's quite discouraging to constantly be looking to others to determine how important we are. We must start thinking and acting differently about other people.

Have you ever felt that twinge of defensiveness when you see another person succeed? We may feel threatened, we may want what another person has, or we may picture our success in place of theirs. "When will it be my turn?"

People need support through their success just as they need support through their struggle. But we're usually unwilling to give it. If someone is at a low we feel compassion and usually reach out. But we see someone who is gorgeous, talented, or doing well it's easy to think they are a threat. When someone is experiencing a high we tend to disconnect, tear them down, or withhold support.

I watched a group of women in their twenties while they were out to lunch. "Wow, you look fabulous," I heard one woman say, followed by, "I hate you." There was uncomfortable laughter. You could feel the tension, but the group continued on looking through the menu as if it were normal to have unspoken hostility.

Think about someone who just bought a new home while you're stuck renting. Think about the person who got the lead in the school play versus the quiet kid who wouldn't even try out. Think about your neighbors who just went on vacation to Europe while you can hardly even afford to pay your cell phone bill.

Think about how a run-down woman looks at a woman who is clicking past in four inch heels, wearing a brand name dress. It typically fills us with resentment, not support.

Why do we hold such quiet hostility toward another person who seems to have an advantage over us? If you do not like another person, it can often be traced to a feeling like our own worth is being threatened.

One-up

Competition is everywhere. The Olympic Games, reality television titles, beauty pageants, and athletics tell us only one can have the prize. Our skills are being tested from little league baseball to the World Cup championship. There is first chair in the orchestra and the lead role in a play. Sometimes that rivalry is translated on a personal level.

We like to label people as most attractive, smartest, strongest, or funniest. Life becomes a contest. We try to be better. We try to out-do others. Most of the time we're not trying to outdo the magazine cover supermodel. We are trying to compete with the people who are closest to us, our sister, our neighbor, and our friends. Social competition is more common within families and friendship circles than it is with someone you don't know personally.

While sitting at the playground one mom started a conversation with another mom. "You got up at six this morning? I got up at five to go to the gym."

"You can do fifteen push-ups? Well, I can do fifty."

"Where did you get that baby stroller? My stroller came from a baby boutique in Hollywood. It's top of the line."

"I made organic pizza last night from whole wheat flour I ground myself."

"You take yoga classes? Well, I take Pilates and kick boxing."

Most of the time, when someone has a conversation with you where they are questioning you and trying to show you how great they are, they are usually feeling intimidated. They see you as someone great and in their own insecurity are trying to let you know they are great too.

Acknowledging people, honoring them, and seeing them is one of the most important things you can ever do. Give people your acceptance. The more acceptance you give other people, the less need you will feel to compete. We need to start seeing self-worth as unlimited. It's not "if she gets it, I won't." Self-worth is abundantly available.

Gossip and drama

After working with teen girls for years, I started to notice a word used a lot: *drama*. Anytime we use the word *drama*, we are really referencing high emotion conflict. If you know what is at the root of it, you can fix it. The core problems of drama are feelings of insecurity mixed with miscommunication. People often start rumors, mind read, make assumptions, and simply don't talk. It can feel scary to directly address another person you think doesn't like you. Instead of talking things out, we tend to react in indirect ways. We talk about other people instead of talking with them. Conflict is part of life. We must learn how to handle it.

From dealing with gossip to being excluded by a friendship circle, there are some skills that we can develop to better handle the drama. Learn how to talk to people directly. Remember that self-worth is constant. See people. Break the mean-girl stereotypes.

Entertainment geared for teen girls is thick with conflict, bullying, gossip, and teens often mimic and model the behavior that they see. Conflict is a part of life. But it is not normal or healthy to handle conflict through verbal abuse, physical abuse, or bullying. Gossip is rooted in insecurity and fueled by entertainment. We must reteach ourselves to communicate and understand people.

When we feel conflict with another person, we often don't understand that person. If we truly knew and understood another person, we would be able to develop compassion and empathy before seeking to get revenge and retribution. The more we build up and encourage others, the more confident we tend to feel. The more we tear others down, the more guarded and insecure we tend to feel. Build other people up. Let another person, especially your rival, be successful and in turn you are going to discover a deeper level of confidence.

The most uttered phrase in the self-help world

It's one the most uttered phrases in the self-help world. "Don't compare yourself to others." I'll be the first to admit I've used this phrase, thinking it was the ultimate solution. It initially seems like the answer. Don't look at your neighbor's life and compare it with your own. Don't take your worst moments and think they should be like another person's best moments. It's the idea that we should stop looking at other people. This advice is not working.

We all do it. We compare ourselves to other

people and feel bad if we don't measure up. We make comparisons because we are just people. Human nature emphasizes self-preservation. Our biggest struggle with others is not in the comparison, it is misunderstanding self-worth. It is allowing the perception of others to make us think we are minimized. This misconception leads to envy, defensiveness, entitlement, inadequacy, and competition.

We are surrounded by amazing people, and if you truly know what self-worth is, you have no reason to let any of these people become a threat to you. Yet it happens. We take the talents, awards, lifestyles, and success of others so personally that we may as well be crying out, "What about me?"

We see someone who has a great outfit on and instead of celebrating how good they look, we may have thoughts like, "I wonder where she got that so I can look fabulous too."

"What about me?"

While sitting through a community choir concert, one woman convinced herself she didn't have any talents, expressing, "I should have let the beautiful music at the concert comfort my spirit, instead all I let myself think was 'I can't sing, I can't dance, I can't perform in front of an audience, I don't play the piano. I'm not a very gifted person.'"

"What about me?"

A stay-at-home mother started to let discouragement set in after watching her neighbor work a high-paying corporate job, while being the mother to five children, while being a volunteer at the school, while maintaining a beautiful home. How could someone with so many responsibilities keep it together better then she could?

"What about me?"

After watching the other neighborhood four-year-olds, one young mother started to feel the pressure to put her child in advanced preschool, piano lessons, gymnastics, and math tutoring to make sure the child had an edge.

One woman watched another coworker get a promotion, complete with a bigger salary and more opportunities. To offset the emotions of resentment, she began to criticize and critique everything she did, just waiting for the promoted woman to do something wrong so she could talk about her flaws to others.

We watch another person display their musical talent. Instead of sincere applause we very quietly think, "I wish I could sing." We watch something good happen in another person's life like marriage, a job opportunity, unexpected money, and we take it so personally. "When is something good going to happen to me?"

Go ahead, look around. You're going to do it anyway. Learn how to do it right. Make the right comparisons.

See the work behind the success

People become more visual during success. We see the achievement before we see the struggle. Effort, hard work, and sacrifice usually happen quietly. We're quick to let another person's success bother us, but slow to see the work and sacrifice they put in.

The next time you find yourself looking at another person and thinking, "What about me? When will it be my turn?" Stop and instead consider what it took for the other person to get to the point that they are. Overnight success stories usually aren't based on someone magically getting their big break. There is a back story. There are hours and hours of diligent unseen work. Start applauding effort. Consider whether you would be willing to work as hard. Start seeing the sacrifice and time that explains another person's success.

Find the similarities

There are core emotions of love, fear, inadequacy, and struggle we can all connect with on some level. Instead of seeing all the things we are not, all the ways we are different, and emphasizing how we're divided, stop. See how we are alike.

If I could flash back to the sixth grade student council elections, it would have made a powerful emotional difference if I could stop feeling bad for myself, stop thinking I was excluded, and instead see what I had in common with any of those other eight newly elected students. I may have found connections, common interests, and common feelings of wanting to fit in. In the process of connecting, I could have seen beyond my self-wallowing and made a friend.

I had a mother approach me in the community and abruptly say, "You've no idea. You don't know what my life is like."

To be honest, I felt defensive. She said that to me on a

particularly tiring day. My first reaction was to lash back, "Oh, yeah? I haven't slept in nine years. I can't remember the last time I went on a date with my husband. I fed my family, but I was so busy I forgot to feed myself. Our hot water heater just broke, and I haven't had a shower in three days." I didn't say it though. It was a good thing because it would have pushed her away, and we both would have left the conversation feeling alone.

We ended up having a good laugh about the struggles of taking a shower when you have kids. She initially looked at me and assumed I don't have any struggles, pain, or problems. She felt alone. I looked at her and wanted to list off all the ways my day was worse than hers. All people struggle. Instead of pointing fingers at one another, we really should look for common ground.

We all know what it feels like to be hurt, rejected, or left out. When we are hurting, don't look for other people who seem to be fine. Instead of trying to push yourself away because you are different seek ways you are like someone else. We have a tendency to cast ourselves out and put up our defenses. When we feel alone, it may be our own fault.

"You have no idea what my life is like."

"I'm not like you."

"We'll never be like the Jensen family."

"You don't understand me."

"Look how hard my life is."

"Everyone else lives a good life but me."

"I'm different."

We are more alike than we know. We have

commonalities if we will look for them. Look at other people in moments of pain and success and see how you can connect. What can you find in common? Imagine what it would be like to have another person there to support you when you've needed it. Use that emotion to share support with others.

Connect with others before excluding yourself. We tend to see all the things we are not. Focus instead on all the things you are. Would you rather outcast yourself for being different or connect for being similar?

Compare to be educated

We would all be socially backwards if we didn't make comparisons. We compare to learn. Think back to your childhood. There is no way you would know what a banana or an apple was if you didn't make a comparison. You compare numbers in math and writing styles in English. Comparisons are part of the educational system. Make comparisons to learn, to understand expectations.

Instead of letting another person's talents threaten us, why can't it inspire us? Look at what other people are doing and use it to get new ideas. Build your knowledge base by seeing what other people are doing. Watch, learn and see new things you are capable of doing.

Celebrate imperfect versus imperfect

Think about the last time you were in a grocery store. It seems like when we make a comparison, we tend to look at the airbrushed magazine picture, not at the people standing in the checkout line. Look around.

We are all okay.

Don't look around to put yourself in a social hierarchy or on a level. Don't tear other people down to build yourself up. Just look around and see people. See these everyday people who are extraordinary, but real. See the mom in her yoga pants with the crying baby. Look at the grandmother who is walking slowly. See her white hair and wrinkles. Look at the pharmacy line, not to make people feel uncomfortable, but simply notice that there are real everyday people with real everyday struggles, just like you.

We tend to feel like everyone is looking at us, but usually everyone is so concerned about what's going on in their own lives. Notice how little you've been thinking about those real everyday people who walk past you in the grocery store.

Make it about them

If you are going to compare yourself to other people, stop making it about yourself. Notice the needs of other people. Recognize what makes them real. If you think your life is boring, worthless, or miserable compared to another person you are missing out. If you are feeling like a loser because you didn't go to college like your neighbor, you haven't written a book like that expert on television, you didn't make the better potato salad at the potluck, you don't drive a new car like your brother, or you didn't get recognized for your interior design like your friend then you are only thinking about yourself.

When you look at the lives of others selfishly you

will feel resentment or arrogance. You are back on the emotional rollercoaster. If you are going to compare, stop being self-centered and start noticing your ability to better the life of another. What are they going through? Even if that means you celebrate the success of another person, think about bettering them. Sincerely practice seeing others, because it doesn't come easy. You have a powerful influence that sometimes gets weakened because you're too busy worrying about yourself.

Perhaps one of the most self-improving aspects of life is when you forget about yourself. This doesn't mean you forget to take care of yourself. It does mean that you let go of what you want so you can help others to get what they want. It is the art of giving up something good for something better and allowing others to take greater priority than yourself.

Confidence is not about being self-centered. It's about being emotionally centered, so you can better see other people. Take the time to reach out to that one person who also matters.

See and celebrate other people

If you want people to care about you, stop and care about them. Stop blaming and start giving people credit. Speak highly of people. If you see something good, share it, vocalize your admiration, give them a boost, support them, and help them to be even more successful.

Sometimes we withhold praise because we feel like it will minimize us. Sincerely praising others is healing. Supporting other people does not take from your significance. It actually has the opposite effect in that the more you support other people, the more your feelings of being supported grow. The more you see and celebrate the self-worth of others, the more you see can celebrate your own. Honor, congratulate, and value the good other people do. Praise the little things. Gush over the big things. Pay attention to, reward, and shout it from the bottom of your toes when someone else is succeeding.

Now that I think of it, isn't it absolutely amazing that there are women who are named the Young-American-Super-Business-Woman-to-Watch-of-the-Year and they do go to Europe to get more ideas to bring back to us?

Understanding Self-Worth

You are enough.
Your ideas are enough.
Your talents are enough.
But you are the one
that needs to figure this out.

Chapter 6

Self-Acceptance

"Can I please be a ballerina?"

After the birth of my third child, my daughter was feeling left out. We noticed she needed some time that could be individually hers. A time where she wasn't being pushed aside when the baby needed attention. After looking at our options, Evalyn had her heart set on taking ballet. She looked at the online pictures of a local studio and said, "That's what I want to do."

We went to the studio to orient ourselves with the class for four-year-olds. As we walked into the waiting area we were greeted by a kind woman wearing a black instructor's leotard with her hair in a bun. She introduced herself, "I'm Ms. Michelle." We toured the facility, received instructions, including a list of Dancer's Manners, and took a minute to chat as the four o'clock class arrived. As soon as we left the studio, Evalyn looked up at me and whispered excitedly, "Mom, my ballet teacher likes chocolate."

Time passed and ballet was always something to look forward to. It was a safe environment where Evalyn felt like she was learning something new and she didn't have to compete with her baby brother. It was significant to her.

It was a spring day when Evalyn came home from a different event with a bag full of candy. To any child's delight, they tend to sift through wrapped packages of chewy, creamy sweets and pick which ones they will eat. Evalyn was no exception. She sat with her candy, sorted through the stash, then gasped.

"Its chocolate! Ms. Michelle loves chocolate."

She pulled out two wrapped packages of the best chocolates and held them up for me to see. "Mom, I must give these to Ms. Michelle."

Ballet was a week away. If she wanted to give that chocolate to her teacher, she was going to have to keep it safe. That's a long time to keep candy safe when you have an older brother. Evalyn was adamant that she could do it. Thoughtfully, she put the two chocolates on the top of her white dresser and protected that candy for an entire week. On the day of class Evalyn dressed in her pink tights and black leotard. Thirty minutes before class started, she carefully held the chocolate with two hands cupped together. Her excited hands enclosed the chocolate until we arrived at class.

Have you ever seen what happens to chocolate when it sits confined in a child's hand? It becomes soft. It sculpted to the shape of her four-year-old fingers.

The studio waiting room had the bustle of students and parents getting ready for class. Evalyn quietly walked over to her busy teacher with her two hands held carefully in front of her. She softly addressed her by name.

"Ms. Michelle. I have a gift for you." Evalyn opened

her hands.

As a mother, I was hoping that Michelle would make eye contact with me, so I could offer an apologetic smile. Fortunately, she didn't. Her eyes were locked on Evalyn's. Michelle kneeled down next to her. She put her two hands alongside Evalyn's two hands.

"I love chocolate," said Ms. Michelle. "It is one of my very favorite things."

Evalyn passed the candy. She rested the now finger-sculpted chocolates into Ms. Michelle hands. She accepted it with care and pulled it to her heart.

"Thank you. How kind that you would share this with me. I love it." Ms. Michelle put her arm around Evalyn, and they walked into class.

I stood in the studio for a moment filled with gratitude at the significance of such a simple act. I've never felt so grateful to see another person receive love. It was a meager, but precious gift. It was powerfully received. It would have been so easy to disregard or fail to see this quiet child who wanted to share her love with a teacher she cared about, someone who saw her, someone who accepted her when she was having a hard time. Giving her teacher chocolate was a way Evalyn could express love. Ms. Michelle's acceptance will always have a tender place in my heart.

Do you have the ability to accept the love and kindness of another person without apology, without justification, without feeling like you owe them, and without feeling inadequate? Think about how you feel when you receive a gift.

Receiving love

The ability to accept and receive love is tied closely to self-acceptance. Love is a scary emotion because it exposes our core, our unprotected soul. It seems we put more time and effort into building walls and protecting ourselves than we do in exposing and opening up. It's scary to have an emotional attachment to someone or something. What if we lose it? It will hurt.

There are many painful aspects of life. The rejection we've faced haunts us. We withhold love because someone else may have withheld love from us. We have a hard time accepting love and letting people in. We turn down someone's offer of help and disregard compliments.

I was once checking out at the grocery store with a cart full of groceries. I had a gallon of milk in one hand and my three kids in tow while pushing a cart. The bagger looked at me with a smile, "Can I help you to the car today?"

"No, thanks." I said. Desperately needing the help, I walked away with my hands full and on the verge of hyperventilating. I had a hard time admitting going grocery shopping with three kids is tough. Even though the bagger could have eased my burden, I was too stubborn to accept his kindness.

Think about accepting a hug or an apology. You receive something that is being offered to you. We accept someone's hug by hugging back. We accept an apology by allowing someone to make things right. We accept gifts by taking them.

Acceptance is a form of approval. It is agreement. It is the ability to receive. It's taking something that is being offered to you. Receiving love is about believing someone when they tell you they love you. It is when you can put your hope for the future before the fear of the past. To better to receive love from another person, you first need to see and feel that love in yourself.

What is self-acceptance?

Self-acceptance is the continual process of learning about our identity, striving for contentment, and recognizing weaknesses without resenting them.

A life without self-acceptance is full of doubt, questions, and anxiety. You have to constantly scramble for approval, for comfort, for security because you cannot generate it yourself. You don't trust. You're indecisive and unsure. It's a very painful and unfulfilling way to live. You have to face the parts about yourself that you don't like.

I'm not telling you to suddenly love everything about yourself. I just want you to be okay. It happens in small steps. It is not a quick process. Pick one thing that you're struggling with today and learn to be at peace with it.

Instead of trying so hard to change, conform, and please others, learn to find acceptance of the life that you have. Try again tomorrow. Stop trying to change yourself into something you wish you could be. Start living the life that you have. Seek peace.

Rejection and fear

Spiders, public speaking, snakes, the dark, what do you fear? Some people are afraid of natural disasters, losing someone they love, commitment, and disapproval. Fear is a survival instinct. The dark is scary because we can't see. We have no control. We don't know what is out there that will hurt us.

If you've ever been asked to stand in front of a group to talk, you've likely felt the anxious rush in your stomach and worried about your ability to say the right thing and what other people will think of you. You don't want to make a mistake. What if you draw attention to your flaws or lack of knowledge? People will talk about you. They will judge you. We don't like to feel judged.

What fears do you need to overcome?

Picture a girl walking with her head down. She doesn't make eye contact. Worried about what others may think, she avoids people. She questions herself, never fully feeling confident. I've met this girl. I've seen her change. It wasn't because of her mom, or her best friend. It was because she was the one who decided to understand self-worth. Slowly she started finding peace with her laugh, her long legs, her light blonde hair, and other things that she could not change. One day at a time she took a trait she didn't like and made peace.

I've watched her, and many others, now walk with her head up. She now smiles and looks at people when they talk to her. No longer worrying about pleasing people, she has overcome the fear of not being enough. She finds contentment in her identity.

You can go from head down and no eye contact to looking up by developing self-acceptance.

Two different homes

Think about visiting two neighbors. Walk into the first house and look around. It could be on a magazine cover. You see a fireplace mantel. It's decorated in ornaments that look expensive. A family picture is on the wall. Pillows line a luxurious couch. You can see the faint lines where a vacuum has been. You wonder if you should take your shoes off as your neighbor ushers you in apologetically, "I'm so sorry!"

She continues apologizing. She's frantic. "Don't mind the mess. I haven't had time to pick up today." She invites you in to sit down and you can see she's clearly upset. You sit very stiffly on the edge of the couch. You carry on a formal and proper conversation and never really sense comfort. You stay on edge. You start to feel judged and wonder, "What would she think if she saw my home?"

Now picture yourself visiting an entirely different home. It is the home of a mother with five children. She opens the door with a smile and simply says, "Welcome to my home. I'm so glad you're here." You feel the sincerity of her words.

As you step inside, you see a simple cozy seating area. There are backpacks on the floor, alongside shoes and socks. You have to move a toy dinosaur to sit, but you find yourself relaxed, sliding back similar to a way you'd sit on your own couch. You have a comfortable real conversation. You feel like you can be yourself.

This experience happened to me. How could an immaculate home make me feel so ill at ease while I was perfectly relaxed in a house some would call messy? I felt unsettled, awkward, and afraid of being judged when I was in the home of someone who was not at peace with herself. When I was around someone who was comfortable, I was comfortable. It gave me permission to be myself.

The home is a very personal place. It is easy to think, "If one thing is out of place in my home, it means I am out of place. If my house is a mess, I am a mess."

It doesn't just happen in our homes. Think about when you are having a night out with friends. Have you ever been around someone who always apologizes for her appearance or make remarks about not looking as pretty as you do? As you listen to the demeaning words she says about herself, does it make you feel a little awkward, uncomfortable? Contrast that feeling. Have you ever met someone who is very real, who sometimes doesn't even wear makeup, and find you feel comfortable around them? You can better be true to who you are.

It's a tale of two homes. You don't need to be perfect to have self-acceptance. You can have peace in flawed circumstances. Self-acceptance is not based on a picturesque life. Peace comes from living the life you have.

The biggest struggle women face

I was recently asked the question, "What is the

biggest struggle you see women facing?" The answer came easily. It's inadequacy.

We focus on the qualities we lack. We focus on what we are not. We may feel like everyone else is better than we are. Inadequacy means we feel less than, we dwell on negative thoughts, we are convinced our efforts are not enough. Inadequacy is a common experience. Everyone will encounter these feeling, yet how we respond to it is different matter.

Feelings of inadequacy may become more intense based on our experiences. Being bullied, teased by peers, having critical parents, recovering from abuse, experiencing neglect, or being treated unfairly tends to amplify these emotions.

We may stay awake at night thinking about what we said and did during the day. We may wish we said something different. We may try to be agreeable or likeable and follow what other people like so that we can be accepted.

We are filled with thoughts that we're not pretty enough, not smart enough, not fun enough, not talented enough. Nothing we ever do, even if it's outstanding, is ever going to be adequate. We can see the worth of others, but we just can't feel it for ourselves.

I've watched people feel like they are constantly coming up short, like they will never be good enough. They apologize, not out of common courtesy, but as a way to protect themselves. They keep a back-up plan in case someone doesn't like them.

I've watched people make self-deprecating comments

in an attempt to get reassurance from another person. We're left responding, "No, you're not useless. You're very talented." We say things like, "No, you don't look fat in that picture, you look very pretty," to try to make them feel better. I've watched people use uncomfortable sarcasm just to hear someone give them a reassuring phrase.

Accountability

We've been conditioned to look for reassurance and messages of self-worth from everyone but ourselves. You must have the courage to forget about every other person and focus on yourself. This message isn't for your friend. I'm not talking to your sister. I'm talking to you.

How are you doing? How is your confidence level? Do you feel like you are a person of worth? Why? What do you need to change so you can heal?

You are enough. Your home is enough. Your ideas are enough. Your talents are enough. But you are the one that needs to figure this out. You already matter. Your mom can't help you, your sister can't make you feel better, and all of your best friend's efforts will be wasted if you don't develop your own strength.

You will burn people out if you don't start taking accountability for your self-worth. You are responsible for yourself, your happiness, and your feelings of inadequacy. You will push people away if you refuse to heal. Any form of validation won't mean anything until you believe it and know it for yourself.

There is nothing more powerful than being around

a person who has accepted their body, character traits, and emotions along with circumstances that cannot be change. Take small steps. Pick one thing you struggle with and simply accept it. Recognize it.

It might be your goofy laugh, the structure of your body, or your heritage. You don't have to suddenly love it. Just be okay. Accept it. Pick another feature and do it again.

Sometimes you must ask another person for help. This emotion of feeling "less than" can become so consuming that the starting point is asking for help, often from a professional counselor. If you need help, ask for help.

You are responsible for your own well-being. You can't blame anyone. Confidence is a choice. One of the strongest forms of peace comes as you take accountability for your choices.

Learn the root problem

So many times when we struggle with something like body image, the problem isn't so much body dissatisfaction as it is fear, and insecurity. It's not about a shape. It's about the need to feel love and acceptance. Consider the root problems of dieting. If your real issue is wanting approval because you were teased in high school, you will never overcome body dissatisfaction by dieting.

Every emotion can be explained. Every hurt has a cause. Discover and soothe the real reason, and you can find long-term peace.

Hard work

There are principles of exercise, work, and self-care that have positive natural consequences. Have you ever seen a woman experience a makeover and think she matters more now than she did before the hair cut and shopping spree? We look at the "after" picture and tend to skip the innate outcomes.

Goal setting gives you purpose and lifts your spirit. Taking care of your body promotes health and happiness. Hard work gives you a reason to live. Work has benefits. Don't disregard positive natural consequences. It's easy to confuse good outcomes with high self-esteem.

One overweight woman spent years feeling bad about herself. She started going to aerobics classes and eating healthy food. Over time she lost eighty pounds. She told everyone, "Being skinny has changed my self-esteem." It wasn't being "skinny" that changed her life. Rather, it was the natural consequences of self-care and hard work that is has positive results.

This woman stopped exercising. She gained the weight back. She expressed, "I have low self-esteem again." The positive natural consequence of hard work and self-care were once again missing in her life.

Lower expectations

"I'm not good enough. I have to be better."

Sometimes we have a hard time with the person we are today in contrast to the person we can become. You can have self-acceptance and still look to the future. Goal setting is important, but it your expectations for your future don't need to make you unhappy about who you are today.

When we don't meet our expectations we can feel frustrated, overwhelmed, and dissatisfied. Give yourself permission to be content. Demand less of yourself. We are told to set goals, and aim high. Sometimes we don't allow ourselves room to make mistakes or rejuvenate because we're so focused on being the best.

During those times you are feeling burned out, lower your expectations. Buy cookies from the store instead of having to make them from scratch. Let your kids make a mess of your living room. Leave the house without wearing makeup. Let go of your to-do list. Stop trying to do so much so perfectly that you don't enjoy life.

See the good

Most people know specifically and passionately what they don't like about themselves, but rarely do we talk about and emphasize the things we like. Develop self-acceptance by pointing out things that are good. What do you like about yourself?

It's hard to point out your good traits. We don't want people to think we like ourselves or something.

I like the lines by my eyes. I know the beauty industry is taking drastic measure to help diminish the look of crow's feet but I love the smile lines that are etched into my skin. It reminds me that I have been happy. I like my stomach. Sure, I've got faint stretch marks and evidence I've had three kids but I like my waistline. My fingers are perfect. Yes, they may have scars on them but, they are just right. My eyelashes are awesome. I have really strong calf muscles.

Our current culture obsesses about perfection. We want to be our best. It's easy to see the good in others and hard to see it in ourselves. What we see, feel, and sense about ourselves functions differently than what we see, feel, and sense about others. Perhaps, just perhaps, that is why it is so hard to see ourselves accurately. We don't get to experience ourselves. And on top of it all we have our crazy out-of-control thoughts to deal with too. What would it be like to greet yourself if you were another person? How do others see your kindness? The way we see ourselves is usually distorted. We experience ourselves through a reflection and our mind.

We've been conditioned to think that admitting we're worth something means we're arrogant. Remember the definition of arrogance and confidence. There is nothing wrong with developing that assurance and speaking openly of it. It becomes unhealthy when we put ourselves above another person. It is arrogance when we start using putting people on a level.

We can point out features we like about ourselves without using a hierarchy, a score sheet, or declaring a loser. It doesn't mean we are better or worse than anyone else

See the good in yourself. Start with your body. What do you like about your body? Create a list of your talents. What is encouraging about your personality? What do you like about your abilities? See the good in your life. What are your blessings?

Understanding Self-Worth

There is a connection between how we laugh and how we see ourselves. Laughing can heal the wounds that our hard work and tears don't.

Chapter 7

The Role of
Laughter in Self-Worth

After spending the cold winter months indoors, people do crazy things to stay entertained. At my house, we dance. The robot, moonwalking, jumps, spins, and pumping fist bumps were a way that my kids and I would cope with the boredom of winter lockdown. We turn up the music and laugh.

As the snow melts and the sun comes out, so does the neighborhood. One lively spring day, I found myself standing in front of the elementary school during the rush of after school pick up. As soon as the clock hits two-thirty, the sidewalks, roads, and parking lots become filled with parents and children. Today was no different. The bell rang. It was an instant flood of people.

Amid the chaos, my daughter Evalyn stepped off the sidewalk into the grass and started dancing, singing, "Boom, boom, wiki-wiki, wiggle, wiggle, jump." It was one of the moves we would do in the basement. I smiled. I figured all the rushing parents wouldn't think twice if they saw a child dancing. Wiggle, wiggle, wiki-wiki, wiggle, wiggle, pow. I recognized a woman from church who smiled at Evalyn as she walked to her car.

Kids were lined on the sidewalk waiting for rides. Parents were walking back and forth. Cars were starting up in the parking lot. Above the noise I heard the words, "Mommy, it's your turn to dance."

"No, thanks. You go ahead."

"But, Mom, it's your turn," she insisted. "You need to dance."

I looked side to side. There were people everywhere. My heart beat faster. I cautiously wiggled my shoulders, and spun in a circle. I quickly looked around to see if anyone noticed me. Evalyn did. She was applauding.

"Mom, you need to dance. This time, ballet style."

What would you do?

Not wanting to disappoint my child, I took first position, did a chassé, and found myself suddenly prancing across the elementary school lawn. I took to that lawn like a fluffy cloud. I was floating, arms extended, leaping with pointed toes. My big finale was the robot complete with a beat box. We laughed.

No one openly ridiculed me. Nothing bad happened. In fact I think everyone else was in such a bustle most didn't notice I was giving a free performance. It really wasn't as embarrassing as I initially thought it was going to be. When I'm in my basement, I don't even think twice about busting a move. It was harder to freely dance in public, right in front of the PTA President. I didn't have the same courage of a child. Feeling self-conscious, I was worried about what other people were going to think.

Being self-conscious

"Who wants to come to the front to be a volunteer?" Picture yourself visiting a kindergarten class. Notice the joy and willingness a five-year-old has to participate. Everyone wants the mystery bag. Everyone wants to be line leader. Every child raises their hand at the opportunity to come to the front of the class to help.

Around fourth grade something changes. There is still willingness, but it's hesitant. We start noticing other people. Middle school and junior high seem to bring out the worst of our insecurities. People tell us to hide. We feel shame. If we're different, we're a target so we try to fit in. People send us messages that we are not good enough. Many people stop wanting to participate altogether. We lose joy. It takes years to recover, and we spend the rest of our lives learning that it's okay to be different.

As I considered dancing in front of the elementary school, I suddenly became hyperaware of myself and everyone around me. In a split second I sensed my heart beat. Looking down at my mom jeans and T-shirt, I wondered if I was wearing the wrong outfit for frolicking. What if someone thought I was frumpy? Channeling my super-hero-super-hearing I noticed the voices of all the people around me. The kid with the red backpack was standing by the curb with his dad. I could still see the mom from church who just walked past. People were going to think I was the crazy mom. They will start talking about me. People will start walking in the opposite direction when they see me. Then I took a deep breath in. I let it all go.

When we feel self-conscious, our lives feel under investigation like a specimen under a microscope.

We act as if everyone is watching us and put extreme thought into everything we do. We become acutely aware of our every action and the people around us. We are nervous, awkward, and uncomfortable. We don't want to do something wrong. Feeling like we're being critiqued, we worry what others are going to think about us. Sometimes we even play these scenarios out. Other people can easily convince us to hide.

Once while standing in front of a group of women, I was about to introduce myself. For the first time I felt courageous enough to admit some of my struggles. "Hi, my name's Karen, and I once went four months without mopping the kitchen floor."

Afterward I had a respected woman pull me aside. "Oh sweetie," she said as she caressed my shoulder. "You don't need to say that out loud."

It would be so easy to listen to the respected woman. My life would be completely different today if I believed her. Sometimes I try so hard to lead others to think only good things about me. It's easy to let the respected woman, my neighbor, the PTA President, the woman from church, or the kid that teased me to cause me to screen everything I say and do. Seeking constant approval is exhausting. I don't want to live in fear of what other people will think. I don't want to try to control how others see me. It doesn't leave room for what I think. There is no way I can be myself if I'm trying to please other people.

Embrace embarrassment

We tend to see embarrassment as a bad thing. What would be different if we made embarrassment good? Feelings of shame could be replaced with the joy of being alive.

In high school I was running to get to my next class. With a heavy backpack and a book in my arms, my toe grazed the step and I tripped. I couldn't catch myself. I rolled upwards like a marble through molasses. Sprawled on the high school steps, I thought my life was over.

While in a long line at the grocery store, my nine-year-old son pulled one of my "little plastic bathroom sticks" out of my purse. With people watching us he yelled to me, "Mom, can I have this?"

During winter when I was in college I slipped on the ice and fell right in front of a boy I thought was cute. I blushed but then I said, "Oh look, I'm falling for you."

I can be mortified or I can be accepting. Embarrassment is good because it is fun, it makes for great stories, it allows us to be real, and it provides us an opportunity to connect with the people around us. In our minds we think that being flawless will bring people to us when really it's the opposite. Perfection usually pushes people away. It's in our most core vulnerable moments we find acceptance and the best connections with others. Embrace embarrassment and you'll find that you can better be yourself and build deeper connections with others.

The Laughter Pivot

We laugh when there is a good feeling mixed with a surprise. It's that outward expression of joy, connection, recognition, and the unexpected. Some of our most connected moments and funny memories come from our most difficult situations. When something goes wrong we can laugh or we can get upset. Choosing to laugh will help us enjoy life and appreciate ourselves. Laughter lifts depression and heals pain.

There are times we wish our lives away. We're focused on the monotony and zone out for another Monday. When we are at home, we think about work. When we are at work, we think about home. When we eat dinner, we don't taste it. We are everywhere but in the present. Laughing can help us stop and see what is happening in the moment.

My grandpa had a gift for making people laugh in everyday situations. Having dinner with him was always exciting. I would usually be eating my potatoes like a zombie and say, "Please pass the salt." My grandpa would zoom the salt right past me.

"There you go," he'd say. "The salt passed right by you."

It always made me smile and snap me into the present.

My brother Greg is good at making our family laugh. I once called home, "Hi Greg, can you grab mom for me?" Waiting for my mom to get on the phone I heard Greg's voice. "Don't worry I got her." He was actually grabbing my mom, Amelia-Bedelia style, by the shoulders.

"I grabbed mom, he said. "Now what do you want me to do with her?"

On a cold, dreary January day my family gathered to sit down to dinner. I had made a pot of soup and placed it on the edge of the table. My toddler reached up and pulled at the pan. Our entire dinner spilled all over the floor. It was exhausting. I had to mop up the soup and figure out what to feed my still hungry family. While sitting down to peanut butter and jelly sandwiches we engaged in our dinner routine of asking the kids the best and worst parts about their day. I asked my fourth-grader, "Spencer, did anything sad happen today?"

"Josh spilled the soup," he said all grumpy. He was hungry and wasn't very happy that it had taken an extra twenty minutes to eat.

"What was the best part of your day?"

Spencer paused and then started to smile, "Josh spilled the soup." He giggled. Evalyn started to belly laugh. Josh, the toddler, saw us laughing and he threw his head back and giggled. Their laughter made me laugh harder. We were mindlessly laughing over the spilled soup.

Laughing can help you enjoy the present. Laughing heals. For a moment we share in the same experience. Laughing can help us through our struggles because it brings joy back in our lives. There is a connection between how we laugh and how we see ourselves. Laughing can soothe the wounds that our hard work and tears don't. When you admit and openly accept your flaws it will build your confidence. Humor is a tool, if used correctly, can make that happen. Laughing brings self-acceptance.

Laughter isn't always good. Humor has a pivot. To one end it leads to happiness, fun, connection, and healing. To another end laughter can be used as a form superiority, contempt, or hurt. We can cling to it like a life raft, desperately trying to hide pain and injure others. Unkindness is socially accepted if it's disguised as a joke. Humor can be used as a weapon or it can be used to heal.

Sarcasm

You are disappointed in tonight's dinner menu and exclaim with contempt, "I love leftover meatloaf."

It's raining. Your plans got canceled. "Best vacation ever."

"Mother of the year," she says after she forgot to pick her child up from daycare on time.

Someone adds more to your workload, and you reply with, "Great."

After you make a mistake, your friend tells you, "You're not the brightest crayon in the box."

We use sarcasm in a variety of ways. So much of it is conveyed in the tone. One of the most recognized forms of sarcasm is when we say the opposite of what we really think. We use ironic words to hide our real feelings. Cutting remarks may be directed at other people or at ourselves.

With sarcasm we can hurt people without appearing as if we mean to. We think we can say anything we want if we follow it up with "Just kidding." Passively, we hide our pain by confusing people with contradictory words. Sarcasm can hurt relationships. We make snide remarks when we do something wrong or when something goes wrong.

There is truth behind sarcasm. It can be detrimental to understanding self-worth because the words you use can be a passive place to hide from what is really bothering you. You might laugh your problems away instead of facing them head on. Making jokes about other people when you feel like they minimize you or if you see opportunity to get an edge over them is a way to cower. Use laughter to heal, not to hide.

Humor damages our relationships when we use it to conceal pain or bring pain into the lives of others. Laughter can improve our relationships when we connect together. Look for positive humor. Associate with people who build you up. Be the person who is accepting and will help others to be their best.

Four ways you can laugh

Misdirection: Comedians use misdirection. They lead you to think down one path, so they can surprise you and get a laugh. Misdirection is the ability to see what others overlook. Using misdirection in everyday life can help ease tension, enjoy the moment, and see things from a new perspective. Life sets us up with routine expectations. Look for the wrong answers. Be the one to see what others don't see.

They can be puns about your vegetables at dinner. Anytime we would eat cauliflower for dinner, my dad would tell me, "Hey, Karen, you're what I call-a-flower."

They can be words you don't expect to hear from your children's mouths. "Mom, he's breathing on me. Make him stop breathing."

It might be an everyday conversation. "Grandma, who is the oldest relative that you can remember?" She replies, "Adam and Eve." You were expecting her to say, "Great Aunt Edna."

While at the grocery store, my brother was holding a package of toilet paper when a girl from school walked past. "This is all for my bathroom."

Be wildly optimistic: Optimism is funny, because it is unexpected. Pick one disadvantage like big feet, frizzy hair, or having age spots. Use a problem or attribute you see as a setback. Create a list of reasons your disadvantage is really an advantage. This will help you develop self-acceptance and find contentment with the attributes you have.

I'm self-conscious about my shoes size. I have big feet for a girl. But there are advantages to having big girl feet. They make you a better swimmer. You can always find your size in the clearance rack. You've got great balance. You can trick your friends into thinking they've found Bigfoot. Who needs expensive equipment rental when you've got your own skies?

If you are struggling to find self-acceptance pick one specific trait that is hard for you. Write it down and come up with ten reasons it really is a positive thing. Don't like your frizzy hair? There are advantages to having frizzy hair. I don't fear lightning storms. Do you have age spots like I do? Age spots are good. They entertain my kids when we are at church. I've got a built in game of connect the dots.

Remember not to hide pain with your laughter. Rather, use these techniques to get your insecurities in the open. Admit them. Accept them. Embrace them. You might start off questioning your optimism and find that thinking positively, at its extreme, leads you to feel more hope.

The mix-up: It is funny to match up two things that don't usually go together. You can pick something you're struggling and match it up with something random. Think of clever and funny ways they are alike. How is high school like a shoe? Conflict is like a sandwich. Being in a family is like going fishing. Imagine your fears in an opposite situation. Describe your life and feelings using a new situation. Don't try to be funny. Just be real. Use specific truth and the humor will follow.

Try it. Create your own. Think of one frustration you have. See it in a new light. A Star Wars character can tell my son to pick up his toenails. Santa Clause takes on the mean girl drama at school. What would it be like if every one-up mom conversation was spoken in whale calls?

Picture the organic-stroller-I-sleep-less-than-you-conversations in the slurred, almost inaudible singing of the majestic ocean animal. It's very healing.

Here's another example to help you out.

"Being a mom is like running a marathon in flip-flops. You're going to put in a lot of effort, yet never cross the finish line."

Apply the Worst Case Scenario: Think about a self-conscious behavior you have and picture the worst things that can happen in that specific situation. Instead of dwelling on this, learn to be okay with the bad outcome. If you can accept the result, you've got nothing to fear. Instead of hiding, we learn to embrace our flaws and face our fears.

Go ahead, test out your social fears. See that your reservations are not as bad as you think. Do something embarrassing on purpose. You're going to find that the things you fear are in your mind. Talk to perfect strangers, dance in the elevator, tell a knock-knock joke to your mailman, or go make an embarrassing purchase at the grocery store. Discover the freedom from letting go of your fears.

I had a friend once dare me to sing a Christmas song in a public location. Singing in public is one of my biggest fears. I can't hit a note to save my life. I stood in a plaza with people frantically walking about and belted out an off-key version of Rudolf the Red-Nosed Reindeer. I even held up reindeer paws. My friends stood on the sidelines and laughed with me. I was initially mortified. I got a few funny looks, but it was nothing like the mental catastrophe I built it up to be. If anything, more good came out of it than bad.

"I get nervous when I am at the gym." One woman shared.

Another woman added, "I worry about what I look like. I'm not very coordinated. It's scary to take a class because I fear what other people will think of me."

I attended a dance-style exercise class with the purpose of helping the women there to stop feeling so self-conscious. I understood the fear of being judged. In a class full of forty people, in a room full of mirrors, with an athletic girl in a sports bra just standing feet away, I'm doing the grape-vine to the right while the instructor is moving left. I'm waving my arms up when they should be down. After thirty minutes of following the instructor we circled up as a class of forty. We tested out a theory.

"What would happen if we accepted the worst thing that could happen in a dance-style exercise class?" What would the worst thing be?"

Some people responded, "Everyone would be starring at you."

"You wouldn't know the routine."

"You look like a fool."

"Now's your chance. Let's test it out. Try standing in front of the room with everyone starring at you. The purpose is to see that it's not as bad as you think." The music started and the instructor got it started. She stood in the middle and set the tone with a coordinated high-energy freestyle dance. She stepped into the circle.

"Who is willing to try?"

For a moment nobody moved. Then, one brave soul entered the center and started dancing. It wasn't as coordinated as the instructor but the entire class cheered. As she stepped back, another came forward, then another. We saw women at all skill levels stand in front of their peers knowing they were being watched.

The support in the room was incredible. No one was criticized. In fact, they were respected and encouraged as they faced their fears.

Sometimes we fear being judged. There are times we don't participate. It's scary. But we can find support, respect, and encouragement instead of judgment by testing our fears.

The joy of life

Life is good. It is so much better when humor is used to help people feel good instead of tearing people down. There is a time and a place for humor. I love to laugh. I need humor in my life as much as I need air and water. There is nothing like belly laughing after a long day, listening to a child's goofy giggle over a slapstick moment, and finding someone to share inside jokes with. The contracting air in my lungs and happiness rounding out my cheeks washes my spirit. Laughing refreshes my soul.

Understanding Self-Worth

No matter how hard you try you cannot make another person understand self-worth. Each individual must come to that knowledge for themselves. Your job is to provide the experience.

Chapter 8

Leadership and Self-Worth

When Evalyn was five, we were watching television together. Suddenly, a very sensual commercial came on. My daughter looked at me and said, "Mom, what's that girl doing with her body?"

Every self-worth technique I could think of started to flood my mind. My first thought was, "Quick, get the statistics. Lecture her!" My heartbeat quickened. "Pull out your old college thesis. She needs the workbook on body image. Show her the pictures of media airbrushing. Tell her what body shapes were desired in the 1800s." I felt frantic and desperately wanted to lecture. "Karen, this is your expertise. Do something. She has to know."

Just as I was about to overwhelm her with my sermon, I looked at her little green eyes. My breath caught. What I know doesn't matter. She won't care about what I know if she doesn't make her own connection. In that moment I had to let go of my experience, so she could have her own.

My five hour lecture was reduced to two sentences. "I don't think that girl knows how cool her body is. Why do you think your body is so good?"

There will come a time in life when you will be in a leadership position. You will play a vital role in helping another person establish self-worth. Do you know what to say? Do you know what to do?

No matter how hard you try, you cannot make another person understand self-worth. Each individual must come to that knowledge for themselves. Your job is to provide the experience.

What leaders can do is create a positive environment, be strong themselves, see another person as they can become, and create an experience where the person you lead can learn for themselves.

Families are powerful. Self-worth starts at home. What a child sees, hears, and feels on a daily basis will become the foundation. A home is the most important and the most powerful place for self-worth leadership. If you're in a family, you're a leader.

Friendships matter. Self-worth is framed and redefined through relationships with peers. Messages, both good and bad, start to flood the foundations that were started at home. You are powerfully influenced by the people you associate with. If you're a friend, you're a leader.

Communities are influential. Youth leaders, teachers, instructors, neighbors, sometimes a child will listen to you differently than they listen to a parent. Your example weighs heavily. If you're in a community, you're a leader.

Don't disregard the impact you will have on people.

Positive environment

Think about a time when you've sat by a friend in a classroom, and you leaned over to whisper something to them. You quietly laugh. You feel connected.

Now, think about being the person on the outside, sitting in a classroom, feeling alone. Watch two people lean together and whisper. You don't know what they are talking about, and it is easy to assume they are talking about you. Even if they are making casual observations, side whispering makes people feel unsafe.

Environment matters. No, you cannot give another person an understanding of self-worth, but you can create a healthy environment. Get to know the difference between a safe versus unsafe environment. Initially when we think of a place being safe, we think of physical protection, like dead bolting the door at night, putting up a baby gate on the stairs, or reminders not to run with the scissors. Safe surroundings are also emotional.

In your home, in your classroom, in your social circles are you helping people feel emotionally protected, meaning their needs for love, respect, belonging, and acceptance are being met? Leaders must also provide good boundaries, expectations, and be prepared to deal with conflict, because if people are going to reach their potential, they must also understand life takes effort. An emotionally safe environment is a place where we can connect with others.

Think about a time where your ideas were disregarded or no one valued what you had to contribute. People will tune out if they feel misunderstood. People will also shut down if they have no sense of ownership. People support situations, environments, and ideas that they help create.

Think about a time where nobody knew about something important going on in your life. Have you ever experienced a lack of support? What did that feel like? When we fail to know what is going on in each other's lives environments can feel unsafe.

A healthy environment for self-worth is a place that is protected — a place where you feel you can be natural, without pretending, without feeling like you have something to prove. A safe environment is one that honors both unconditional worth and unconditional support. Healthy environments have powerful communication, a sense of acceptance, and little tolerance for being exclusive. It's a place where people are recognized and respected no matter how different they are.

While growing up my mom and dad frequently communicated that no matter what I had a place there. I was loved always, forever, no matter what. It helped me to be myself. Generate trust. Find ways to show the people that you lead you already have confidence in them. Let them see and feel you value them, so they don't need to impress, please, or prove their self-worth to you. It will allow them to be themselves.

I was once asked to attend a board of directors meeting that served a group of professionals who constantly dressed up in their business best. At one specific meeting I was sent the following message, "No need to dress up, wear something comfortable." The most powerful line was the one that followed. "We all already impress each other."

It was such a simple comment, but it set up trust and acceptance. This note was less about what to wear and more about group acceptance. So often we go into social or professional gatherings with the same pressure as the first day of school—pressure to prove we matter. What would happen if in our interactions with the people we lead started off with communicated acceptance? How can you take away the pressure for people to prove their worth?

You can create a safe environment by being there. Be there to talk, listen, and love one another. Know what is going on. Create that atmosphere of love and safety. Be the refuge. Be the place they can come and feel protected from judgment. Learn about their day. Ask about the good and the bad. Know their hopes, dreams, and fears. Think about ways you can better communicate your confidence.

Be strong yourself

One of the best things you can do for the people you lead is to be strong and take care of yourself.

A forty-five-year-old mother of three we will call Emily was struggling to know she was a person of worth. She lived a life of constant dishes, laundry, watching over her teenagers, and taking care of everyone else. She struggled with body image and never took the time to care for herself. She wore the same clothes she had in her closet for twenty years, she didn't make time for things she enjoyed, and even getting her hair cut was too inconvenient.

Motherhood demands sacrifice. Emily was constantly giving up something nice for herself to better the life of her husband and children. But it was to an extreme. She didn't know how to balance self-care with the demands of her family life.

Sacrifice, even with good intentions, can become unhealthy. Sacrifice, especially when you are caring for another person, can go too far. Sacrifice, even if you are trying to give others the best, can become an excuse to hide your own raw emotions. There are times we sacrifice because we don't understand our own self-worth. You are not supposed to neglect yourself to better the life of another person.

After telling a friend she never went shopping for herself, Emily said, "I can't even stand to look in a mirror. I don't like what I see. I hate my body. "

"Emily, wait," her friend said. "How would you feel to hear your daughter say those exact words?"

Emily's voice cracked. As she wiped away tears, she said, "I wouldn't want my daughter to feel this way. I wouldn't let her talk to herself like I talk to myself. I would correct her. I would tell her what she means to me."

"Why do you do it?" her friend asked. "Why is it so hurtful to care for yourself?"

"I don't know," she first said. "I don't like myself. It's easier to avoid myself."

There is a difference between service and personal

neglect. A mother tirelessly caring for her children, the friend who stepped in to help another get though severe depression, a grandmother reaching out to a grandchild in need, a woman fighting for her cause, a husband working overtime, there are many examples where a person can overlook their own needs. It makes us feel guilty to stop and put ourselves first when other people need us. It's not selfish, it's vital. If you do not take time to strengthen yourself, you will have less to give to others.

Being strong yourself is about staying rested, cared for personally, and being the example. Live how you expect the people you care about to live. You can't expect your friend who is battling depression to stop being self-critical when you are being self-critical. As a mother, you shouldn't tell your daughter she is beautiful inside and out then turn to your own mirror and berate yourself. Are you living in a way you want your child, friend, niece, or neighbor to live?

Self-worth leadership starts with emulating what you are trying to teach. A daughter will watch her mother's relationship with shopping, makeup, gossip, and dieting. Those actions teach her more powerfully than any one conversation. Live your message.

See them as they can become

On the nights we had spaghetti as a preteen, my mom would ask me to make breadsticks. She would praise me. "Karen, you make the world's best breadsticks. Will you make your famous breadsticks for dinner tonight? I love your breadsticks." I believed her. I felt deep in my heart that I was capable of being a world-class baker. I had the confidence to test the recipe and try new toppings.

Now that I look back, my breadsticks were a little flat, crunchy, and they needed salt. I could probably argue my mom may have just wanted help making dinner, but as I reflect on it, she was very strategically trying to see me as I could become. The words my mom told me not only helped me see what I could do in the kitchen, but they helped shape the confident individual I am today.

Someone once argued, "Aren't you worried you'll make people delusional by telling them they're better than they are? Doesn't that set them up for unrealistic expectations?"

My response was "I would rather have a child that errs on the side of greatness than fail to build them up because of fear of what others will think. I want a child that believes in themselves. If that is going to happen, sometimes they need to see what someone else things they are capable of." Believe in the potential of the people you lead. Don't be afraid to make bold predictions about their success.

In the self-help world, there is a popular concept about envisioning the life that you want. If you want to travel, you write your goal as if it's already happened, "I'm glad that I visited Hawaii this year." Take this concept and apply it to the people you lead. You don't deceive them. You talk to them and revere them as if they are the person they can become.

Take time to look for the good in each other. As families spend a lot of time together, it can be easy to get hung up on our bad habits, focus on tendencies, and label one another. Don't get stuck on labels. Mary is shy, Ryan is athletic, or Kim is talkative. Yes, it is good to share when someone does something good, but don't limit one another. Even if someone in your family is shy, don't keep dwelling on that label.

This is one reason why friends and neighbors are so powerful. They have a different perspective of you than your family does. They can help you to see beyond what messages you are receiving at home, reinforce the positive messages, and see continued opportunities for greatness.

Learn for yourself environments

Picture two dirty cereal bowls sitting on the table.

It was a scene I dealt with for years, the dirty bowl with milk splashed about and stray flakes littering the table. Whether it was the aftermath of shredded wheat or the unwanted mateys—because someone picked out all the marshmallows—every morning I would take the bowls to the sink and scrub the milk off the table because I love my kids.

One morning while clearing the cereal bowls from the table, it hit me. Is all this service I perform for my kids really hurting them in the long run? I was focused on what I can do for my kids. What really matters is what I teach them to do for themselves.

Love is not doing everything for them. It is letting them do it themselves. When they are adults, are they going to benefit more from a mom who cleared the table or a mom that taught them how to clear the table?

"If I don't help them in every way I can possibly can, they won't feel loved or find success." So many parents and leaders step in and do too much. It's hard not to feel like our efforts will make our children successful. In doing so much for the people we love, sometimes we take away their experience and ownership. They check out. They don't care. They don't feel anything or learn for themselves. They don't develop the skills they need. We must put more experiences in their hands.

If you want another person to develop self-worth, your role is to provide experience. Provide a moment where they can feel something for themselves. Doing an action for another person will not teach anything. Telling another person can help if they are receptive. But words mean very little if they are not personalized to the one you are trying to help. The most powerful thing you can do to help another person understand self-worth is to create experience. They must participate, think, and feel for themselves. They must gain their own knowledge.

When I got a new cell phone, the settings someone else put on there for me made me feel confused. But when the phone was in my hands while someone talked me through the features, I connected. I understood and knew how to use them.

My children are individual human beings with a mind and spirit of their own. Although I influence them, they ultimately make their own choices. This is a difficult thing to know that as a parent, I am not in control. But I influence powerfully.

It's hard. You can't do it for them. You shouldn't manipulate them. No matter how hard you try, you cannot give your knowledge, your own experience, or your understanding of self-worth to another person. But you will powerfully influence them. You can create experiences for them. You can help them feel how much they matter to you.

Words

If you want to help build the worth of another person, you must pay attention to the power of words. There are words that build another person up and words that tear down. Notice the words you are using to teach.

Make it about them

People tune out if they feel like what you have to say isn't about them. Your own stories and personal examples mean very little unless you can make it about them. One things you can do is change your "I" statements to "you" statements. Here are two sentences.

"When I look in the mirror, I think . . ."

"What words do you think when you look in the mirror?"

Can you see the difference? The first statement is self-centered. The second statement is about them. People will only listen to "I" statements if they are receptive. As you make it about them, it makes them more receptive. Yes, we influence others by talking about ourselves. We need examples in our lives. But be mindful that in sharing those examples, you turn it back to them, and don't get so caught up in your own memories you fail to let them make their own. Try again. Look at these two statements.

"I think it's important to have self-acceptance. I am going to teach you about self-worth."

"Think about a time someone made you feel inadequate. You are going to learn about self-worth."

You might be very excited to share how you discovered your own self-acceptance, but the first statement leaves room for people to tune out. Change the language to make it about others instead of yourself, and you'll better get through to people. Stop talking about yourself and start talking about them.

What is a concept you are excited to share? What are you passionate about? Almost all concepts we deeply care about come because we have had our own experience. It's personal. It's powerful when you have gain knowledge for yourself. Yet when we want to share our passion we often do not let another person have an experience because we have a tendency to tell them about it in self-serving ways.

If you are using words to create an experience, the best thing you can do is work in reverse order. It's human nature to want to spill out good news at the beginning.

"I just learned self-worth is unconditional."

This phrase is good news that a teacher may want to shout out right when a class starts. But this phrase alone won't mean anything unless another person can have time to make it personal.

First make it about them, then share your message

after they have been reflecting on their own life.

Praise

We all need words of encouragement. We can break down praise into three general categories.

Worth Statements: Comments that reflect unconditional love and value. A child, friend, or student does not have to do anything to earn this praise. They should know that they are a person of worth just because they are a person. You can never, never, never use too many worth statements.

"You are amazing."

"I love your smile."

"You have beautiful eyes."

"You are loved."

"You make me happy."

"I love you always and forever, no matter what."

Purpose Statements: Praise that revolves around skills or ability. Children need to develop a sense of purpose, and they will need encouragement as they develop their talents. Sometimes these statements often provide a sense of conditional worth. If they are only hearing purpose statements, the child may feel as if their worth depends upon performance. Purpose statements should be used with care and awareness. They can be used in conjunction with worth statements to reiterate that there are no conditions to being valued as a person. Sometimes unspoken messages are just as painful, just as haunting, as if you heard the words that you're not good enough. Look for ways your child's talents and traits influence, inspire, or make a difference. Tell them. We need feedback when it comes to our achievements. Don't withhold it. Don't overdo it. Know your child and share to help them.

"Great job scoring 100 percent on your math test. You are brilliant."

"You are great at playing the piano. Your music helps calm me down."

"You are great at making friends."

"I love watching you play basketball. Your team really benefited from your talents."

Comparison Statements: These are expressions that gauge, rate, or compare. These statements often put the child above, below, or alongside another person. There is a difference between praise with a good comparison and praise with an unhealthy comparison. Your child should feel like you are their biggest fan. It's incredible to have someone cheering you on.

The main difference between good comparison versus unhealthy comparison is how personal it is and what kind of recognition pivot you use. Praise and opinions should be used to make your life better and not to be the source of worth. To do this well, use an extreme comparison. Use someone they are unattached to like George Washington instead of the child next door. This can help them from feeling in competition with their peers. Remember that putting yourself above or below another person can lead to arrogance, entitlement, or inadequacy. But we still need to hear that we are great in someone's eyes.

Good Example: "You are the most beautiful girl on the planet." See the extreme comparison.

Bad Example: "You are prettier than Emily." Any statement that creates a hurtful hierarchy should not be used. Though you may have good intentions on helping your daughter feel pretty, these statements actually create an insecure child.

Good Example: "You're the best."

Bad Example: "You are better than Lindsay."

Don't minimize their struggles

"Mom, high school is so hard. Kelsey isn't talking to me."

The mother replied, "In ten years this won't even matter. There are bigger problems than your teenage drama."

"This is so hard," replied another young mother to an aunt. "My husband is always gone, and my two kids are exhausting me."

"Oh, that's nothing," the aunt says. "When I was your age, I had four kids. You think two kids is rough, try raising four."

There are many times we don't honor people. We minimize their struggles because we have a feel like we have a better perspective, we're trying to redirect them, or we feel like their struggle minimizes ours. Instead of helping them through their problem, they shut down. They stop trusting us. They don't feel emotionally safe.

"It's not that big of deal."

"High school doesn't even matter."

"This will all be over and you'll look back on this

and think it's stupid.

Honor people. Treat their sincere needs and struggles with care. Sometimes we just need someone to see us, know that we are struggling, and understand us. Instead of brushing away a struggle they are facing, try exploring the struggle or simply letting them know you are listening. If you want to help them, share an experience with them or redirect them, but first let them know you understood them.

Use reflective questions

When I wanted to give my daughter a five-hour lecture on body image, it was reduced to the question, "Why do you think your body is so good?"

She initially responded by saying, "I don't know."

But I could see a light in her countenance. She started thinking. She then answered her own question as I listened to her and helped her recognize her body is good. This is learning that she'll need to keep up on for the rest of her life.

A great way to help someone have an experience is to use reflective questions or give them specific moments in their own life to think about. Personalize it. If you are going to influence another person, you can manipulate them or you can inspire them. To lead people is to see them.

Understanding Self-Worth

What you think about
and focus on will impact
what you see.

Chapter 9

The Most Powerful Skill

My husband and I went hiking up a steep trail in the Rocky Mountains in Utah. Part way through the hike, I got very tired. The elevation was making my lungs burn, my face red, my legs ache, and my fingers swell. I was gasping for breath and started to look down at my feet.

"I don't want to do this anymore," I thought. "This is too hard."

I looked at the brown dirt and wanted to give up. One painful step at a time, I kept going. I was only focused on the steps I was taking. Once white, my tennis shoes were now covered with dust from the trail. It hurt. The rocks were gray. I was exhausted. Every now and then I stepped over a dry stick. It was lifeless. This hike was hard, and I wanted to go home.

It wasn't until I got to the top that I looked up. I gasped. The colors went from dreary to stunning. I could see. Looking out, the view extended for miles. Distant mountains were purple with streaks of jade. I looked to where I had been climbing and could see the bright green trees that lined the trail. The blue sky had gorgeous silver clouds that framed the sun. I watched a butterfly land on a yellow flower. I could see. My perspective changed from exhaustion to a feeling of gratitude and beauty. I missed the best parts of the hike because I was only looking down.

What you think about and focus on will impact what you see. There are times you will miss seeing the things that are really in front of you. There is nothing more harmful to a person's sense of worth than an uncontrolled mind. There is nothing more dangerous to your identity than distorted thoughts. The most important, most powerful, most results-oriented self-worth skill you will develop is mastering your thoughts.

The self-worth fallacies

"I'm such a loser."

"When I lose twenty pounds, then I'll be confident."

"If my house is a mess, then I must be a mess."

"It doesn't matter what I wear because it's never going to be good enough anyway."

"I'll never be a talented as Amber."

"She thinks I'm stupid."

"Nobody wants to hear what I have to say."

These statements are all fallacies. They are incorrect beliefs that could be put through a true-or-false test and all be proven false. Fallacies are commonly used and designed to look true. They are persuasive, camouflaged, and widely unknown. But they are vitally important to your emotionally well-being.

In my English class I learned about something called a hasty generalization. My instructor warned me not to use false statements in my writing. "Everyone likes orange juice" can be proven false. "All women love shopping" is an incorrect phrase. You can't assume an outcome will be true for everyone. They taught me how not to use hasty generalizations in my term paper, but they didn't tell me I should apply it to the thoughts I have about myself.

Low self-esteem is ultimately distorted thoughts about self-worth. It is by recognizing those thoughts that you will be able to spark change that can heal yourself and your relationships. Start paying attention to what you think about. Your thoughts directly create to the emotions you feel. If you want to master anxiety, depression, inadequacy, or perfectionism, you must master your thoughts.

It starts by paying attention. You cannot let your thoughts run wild without emotional consequences. Every emotion can be explained. Figure it out. Pay attention to what you are thinking. If you are anxious, you're probably worrying about the future, anticipating something bad happening, or thinking the words, "What if . . ."

I was recently awake in the middle of the night feeling really low. I was staring at the dark ceiling, and my mind was running wild. I noticed feelings of depression had been creeping in throughout the week. I stopped to pay attention to what was running through my mind. I discovered a series of self-worth fallacies that were at the root of my despair. I replaced my false thoughts with true thoughts and it improved my emotions. The atmosphere in my entire home changed. Learn the self-worth fallacies.

Idealistic Happiness: You assign your happiness or value as a person to an appealing circumstance. "I will be happy when I am skinny."

Comparison Exclusion: A fallacy that originates from ranking your abilities next to another person while making a statement that excludes you from being a person of worth. "I have no talents."

Personal Blame: You blame yourself for something that is not entirely your responsibility or something beyond your control. "Josie's getting bad grades in school. I'm a bad mother."

All-or-nothing Thinking: You don't allow explanations, variations, or exceptions. These statements often use the words always or never. "Nobody ever appreciates me. I never get consideration."

Should Expectations: You focus on things you should be doing and overlook the things you already do. "I should be volunteering."

Labeling: You assign a name to yourself. "I'm stupid."

Mind Reading: You assume people are reacting negatively to you and that you know what another person is thinking. "She thinks I'm a loser. No one wants to be around me."

Making Predictions: You woke up late. You decide it's going to be a bad day. You use one bad moment to base the results of everything else. "My alarm clock went off late so it's going to be a terrible day."

Assumptions: You often believe things must be

completely good or entirely bad, and forget about the other possibilities. A friend calls and cancels your night out. "She doesn't want to spend time with me." You may be overlooking your friend's schedule and life demands.

Emotional Generalizations: A fallacy where you take something you are feeling and assign an outcome. "My house is a mess, so I must be a mess." Another example, "I feel fat, so I am fat."

Master your thoughts

We jump to conclusions, exaggerate problems, dwell on negative, and put labels on ourselves. Anytime you are feeling low or worthless, specifically pinpoint what you are thinking. Recognize the words. Test them out. Can they be proven false? Start recognizing the false thoughts you have and replace them with something that is true.

"Nobody likes me." Stop convincing yourself you're not loved. Notice it can be proven false. Change it to a true statement using the concepts you are overlooking. "My mom likes me. My friend Erica likes me."

"I'll never be as talented as Amber." This can be proven false and uses such an extreme that it is disguised to look true. Stop mindlessly allowing yourself to believe you are counted out by Amber's talents. See the abilities you do have. "I'm good at baking. I'm a good friend."

"He thinks I'm stupid." There is no way to know what another person is thinking. Even if they tell you what they are thinking, you have no control over it, so let it go. "I'm smart. I know how to read. I know how to crochet. I cut hair."

"I'm fat." This is a label. Don't label yourself. It's limiting and an incorrect form of thinking. Replace it with "I'm going to take care of my body. My body is good. My body is strong. I have great eyes. My hands help me."

Starting training your mind to notice distorted thinking and immediately replace the words with truths you are overlooking. Living the true definition of self-worth will produce change.

Think about others

If you are going to master your thoughts, you must develop the ability to see others. You are not alone, and if you ever feel that way, stop and look, truly look, at the people around you. Think about them. Think about their struggles. Think about how you can build their self-worth. Our own understanding of self-worth becomes clear as we think about the self-worth of others. People are strengthened most when they reach out and see another person.

As you start thinking more positively about yourself, you will experience change. But true success is not found when you are thinking about yourself. The best moments in life are when you are strong enough to think about the self-worth of others. Seek for others the self-worth you most want to feel.

Even though self-worth is simple, our lives are complex. Even though our value is constant, we need to be continually reminded. It takes constant effort. We all need someone in our lives that can see our worth on the days that we don't. We need a friend like Haley from high school who reminds us that we all have struggles and nobody is perfect, but we can do our best. We need that ballet teacher who accepts our love. Isn't it incredible if you have a neighbor who can usher you into her home with no apology, where you feel you can be yourself? We need a grandpa to pass the salt just to see our smile. We need that mother figure in our lives who tells us we make good breadsticks. Be that person. Be the one who builds the confidence of others.

Author's Note

I have many dear friends who practice a variety of belief systems, from agnostic beliefs to those with a Christian faith to those who are Jewish and Muslim. I have had conversations about existence with each of them. The views you have on Deity will impact how you feel about your identity. Faith can be a powerful means for answers to worth and purpose. I considered adding another chapter to this book about understanding self-worth through the study of religion and spirituality.

I have studied religion for myself. I love my belief system. It's something that brings me great happiness. Yet I feel there is something invaluable about your individual study of religion. Your personal study will mean more than having another chapter in this book about what I believe happened before I was born and what will happen when I die. Take time to study the worth of a soul in terms of why you exist and where you are going.

Vital answers to why you matter, why you have unconditional value, can be answered through religious study. Ask your own questions and seek out your own answers.

About the Author

Karen Eddington's identity research started in 2002 when she worked with five hundred high school students to learn about their struggles with body image as part of her college thesis. Karen has surveyed women, founded a non-profit self-worth outreach center, and continued research like The Under Pressure Project. Karen's research has lead to the development of The Identity Grid and The Pivotal Eight. Although Karen is most recognized as a self-worth analyst, she is also a family comedian. She uses laughter to help people heal. Karen has been featured on ESPN for helping cheerleaders break stereotypes and is the author of *Today, I Live.* Karen would tell you her real talents are catching throw-up like a ninja, pulling Mr. Potato Head's lips out of the electrical socket, and getting a family of five in the car.

www.kareneddington.com